ITALY

BY INGREDIENT

ITALY
BY INGREDIENT

ARTISANAL FOODS / MODERN RECIPES

VIOLA BUITONI

PHOTOGRAPHS BY MOLLY DECOUDREAUX

RIZZOLI
NEW YORK

New York · Paris · London · Milan

dedication

Per Mimmi di Mamma—che è arrivato e ha rubato tutte le condizioni che avevo sempre posto all'amore

To Mimmi di Mamma—who came along and stole away all the conditions I had ever placed on love

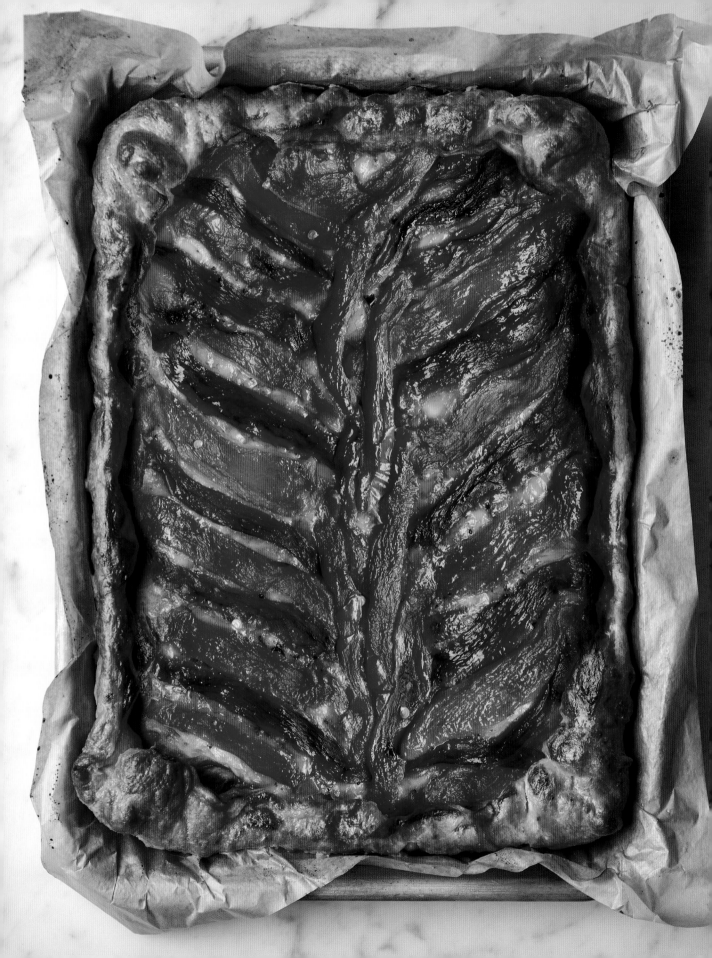

Table of Contents

Introduction

My name is Viola Buitoni. Thank you for choosing to cook with me.

Before you even ask: yes, like the pasta. I am the sixth generation of an Italian family that made food history. In 1857, Giulia and Giovanbattista Buitoni took over a small pasta shop in the Tuscan town of Sansepolcro, near the Umbrian border, and within a generation, they had become the first in the country to mechanize the making and distributing of pasta. In 1907, my great-grandfather invested in the talent of Luisa Spagnoli and her small confectionery shop, which went on to become Perugina Chocolates. Alas, my four siblings and I, all born in Rome and reared in the Umbrian countryside, were destined to be the last generation of the family's entrepreneurial history. The Buitoni and Perugina brands have belonged to Nestlé since 1989.

I am also the daughter of food-loving parents who believed raising your own food was a better way of eating. I was weaned on extra-virgin olive oil and parmigiano. I first spooned ricotta into my mouth straight out of the warm whey in which the local shepherd had just cooked it. I played hide-and-seek in the room where pancetta and prosciutto were hung to cure. At the end of adult dinner parties, I emptied wine leftovers into vinegar barrels I could barely reach.

Our home was a fifteenth-century former convent surrounded by an olive grove. Produce on the table came from our vegetable garden, chickens and fresh eggs came from the coop. In November, we picked olives. In January, a team of *norcini*—the legendary cure masters of Umbria—spent a week at our place slaughtering and butchering our pigs and curing the meat.

Seasonal foraging expeditions were the norm. My siblings and I knew that yellow leaves meant we'd soon be digging mushrooms and shaking chestnut branches, that violets and wild asparagus signaled Easter, that after a summer storm we'd collect snails, and that blackberry picking meant the start of school was around the corner.

Our lives moved to the clock of food.

Whatever didn't come from our land, my parents carefully purveyed from selected food artisans all over the country. Our trips were always dotted with stops to acquire hyperlocal ingredients that could not be found outside their area of production.

When I moved to the United States, many of the ingredients intrinsic to Italian cooking were available. I may not have had warm ricotta, but I could still find pantry staples without which I had no conscious memories. These foods have remained the half of my culinary basket that transformed every new house into a home. The other half of that basket has changed with my place of residence, coloring my Italian cooking with new brushstrokes.

Barely out of college, I chose food as my profession. I have worked in restaurant kitchens, catered to New York's fashion elite, and owned an Italian food shop. Today, I teach home cooks the everyday art of Italian food. Twice a year, I move my classroom to Italy, and lead small groups along unbeaten food pathways, through natural beauty and timeless art.

My work has given me a deeper culinary understanding and technical knowledge of Italian artisanal foods. I have met the people who produce them and have learned to discern their markers of quality. I have seen firsthand their role in the well-being of local communities and economies.

The sum of my stories and experiences taught me to cross local agricultural bounty with the dish-defining taste of Italian artisanal foods, in both my personal and professionals lives.

MY BOOK

For the home cook who must budget time but does not want to give up great flavor, *Italy by Ingredient* is a guide to folding the robust character of Italian pantry staples into everyday cooking.

Each chapter is dedicated to a single ingredient, such as balsamic vinegar or *bottarga*, or to more ingredients with affinity, like parmigiano reggiano and pecorino romano, the pillars of Italian cheese royalty. Take the time to read each chapter introduction, it will make you a more informed cook and consumer.

The recipes' headnotes are personal musings dressed with cooking tricks and tips for ingredient substitutions and other adaptations. The recipes are attainable for cooks of every skill level and, for the most part, not time-consuming. We all have a life outside of cooking to which we must tend.

I convey techniques in a sensorial and understandable language, describing the movements you should make and guiding you through the physical sensations that say you are on the right track. Hold on to those sensations; they will change the way you stand by the stove.

HOW I SHOP

I find my fresh ingredients from local grocers and farmers' markets. For all of the Italian food crafts, I have compiled a list of recommended producers and shopping sources, which appears at the end of the book. I receive no monetary compensation from anyone I mention. I just really like what they make and/or sell, and I have confidence in their practices.

HOW I MEASURE AND SEASON

In the recipes, I have primarily used US standard measures (spoons, cups, ounces, and the like) followed by their metric equivalents. In a few recipes, I have used only US and metric weight measures, as they are needed for a good result.

Salt and pepper are almost always added to recipes as needed. Salt often shows up multiple times in a recipe method. In those instances where it is quantifiable, I have included the amount. But when it comes to correct seasoning, I stand by my empirically tested conviction that sensitivity to salt and spice is subjective. A dish must first and foremost suit your palate. Taste your recipe at different stages and adjust the seasoning accordingly.

To find the salt sweet spot for your palate, you can also rely on the connection between mouth and nose. Smell your cooking before salting it; your nose will find it pleasing. Stir in some salt, sniff again, and note the changing engagement between the food and your olfactory response. When your nostrils are thrilled, your palate will follow suit.

Nearly all of my recipes call for simply salt and pepper, which is sea salt and ground black pepper in my kitchen. Some recipes specify white pepper and occasionally I call for freshly ground pepper for finishing a dish.

HOW I COOK

My cooking is built on the wisdom of those who came before me; I hold and recognize their influence always. I step up to the stove with senses lit. I listen, I smell, I touch, I watch, I taste. My hand in the kitchen is intuitive; it relies on good ingredients. I always listen to my palate—I only cook what I like and want to eat. I rarely shop to the recipe; I start with the season, then build with the flavors that are the characters of this story I am sharing with you. My hope is that I have told it well enough that you can become a confident and excellent modern home cook.

A FEW WORDS ON . . .

European Union (EU) Quality Seals

In 1992, the European Union established guidelines to safeguard foods whose qualities are intrinsically linked to their area of production to discourage imitation and curb fraud. The regulations protect the welfare of communities, producers, and consumers, locally and throughout the world. The steps to obtain one of the three quality seals outlined by the EU are arduous and strict, and rules are enforced by independent organizations. They must first be requested by regions and/or countries and subsequently by the producers. At the writing of this book, Italy claims well over three hundred of the sixteen hundred foods the EU has sanctioned globally.

DOP/PDO DENOMINAZIONE DI ORIGINE PROTETTA/PROTECTED DENOMINATION OF ORIGIN Raw materials, origin, and process stand on the same plane of significance and pristine quality. Before they enter the market, items in this category must have been born and lived in a carefully delineated area. As an example, a PDO cheese must be made only with milk from certain dairy cow breeds raised in a specific way and by licensed dairies. The cheese must also be produced and aged in that same area.

IGP/PGI INDICAZIONE GEOGRAFICA PROTETTA/PROTECTED GEOGRAPHICAL INDICATION For this second seal, in which blue stands in place of red, raw materials come first, followed by process, then origin. In this case, the cheese would still be made with milk from specific breeds, but there would be no requirement on where the milk comes from, and the production process would be less strict; for example, the use of frozen instead of fresh milk. Only part of the product's premarket life needs to be in a designated area.

STG/TSG SPECIALITÀ TRADIZIONALE GARANTITA/TRADITIONAL SPECIALTY GUARANTEE The TSG brand looks like the PGI minus the intersecting curves. For this relative newcomer, process supersedes origin. An example of this category is mozzarella. As long as you don't make it with the milk of an opossum or an alpaca and lace it with garlic and goji, you can request that it be recognized as a TSG.

Common Pantry Items

- Butter is always unsalted.

- Deep-frying oil should have a neutral flavor and a high smoke point, which is why I do not deep-fry in olive oil. If you can find it, rice bran oil is my number-one choice. Canola and sunflower are good alternatives. I do not use peanut oil because of the allergenic potential.

- Flour is unbleached all-purpose, unless otherwise specified.

- Herbs are fresh. Any exception will be indicated in the ingredient list.

- Olive oil is always extra-virgin. Although there are exceptions, this general localization is a good guide for buying your Italian EVOO. Oils above Emilia-Romagna tend to be more delicate and floral; they last on the tongue and nose, and they make you think of jasmine and early-season stone fruit. In central Italy (Tuscany, Umbria, Marche, Abruzzo, and Lazio), we are used to very personable olive oils. They seal your throat with a little spicy pinch and have the long, slightly puckery persistence of an artichoke. Southern olive oils are round, intense, and jammy. Always big bodied and sometimes a little bitter, they coat your cheeks and tongue.

- Pasta for the purpose and philosophy of this book refers to dry. Packages of dry pasta commandeer 20 percent of my pantry shelves. I have enough opinions about pasta to fill a multivolume opus, hence the decision of not giving it its own chapter in this book. Almost every Italian region produces good pasta, though I am partial to Puglia, Abruzzo, and Campania. In the last decade, a number of US artisans are turning out excellent pasta. After reading the label, look at the pasta; its surface should feel rough and look blurry. A sleek pasta will stay divorced from the sauce.

- Red chili flakes—or *peperoncino* in Italian—are a very common seasoning in Italian cooking, but they tend to be milder compared to what is found in many other cuisines. If you enjoy a little fire, you will need to err on the side of abundance when cooking from this book.

SECTION I

CONDIMENTI /
CONDIMENTS

CHAPTER 1

ACETO BALSAMICO / BALSAMIC VINEGAR

A much-misunderstood ingredient with historical roots and a modern nature

I was six or seven the first time I tried real balsamic vinegar. My parents were attending some glamorous to-do in Bologna and had taken my sister Silvia and me along. Our done-up mamma and papà went to their soiree and left our dinner in the care of the hotel's restaurant staff. During the cheese course, what looked like drops of dark silk satin were sparingly dripped over parmigiano. I was hooked. A bottle of this wonder came home with us to Perugia, and *aceto balsamico tradizionale* (traditional balsamic vinegar) became the treasure in our pantry we only shared with close friends.

Nowadays, if I had a penny for every time I've heard the word balsamic, I'd be happily retired and pursuing other passions. We all love it. We all use it. But what, exactly, makes vinegar a true balsamic? And why can a bottle of it go for anywhere from $3 to $300?

The answer to the first question is process and origin. Traditional balsamic vinegar is made from grape must, the juice that grapes release on first pressing. The must is cooked, then steered through a process of acetic fermentation and finally aged. No other ingredient is added. Traditional balsamic originates within the borders of the provinces of Modena and Reggio Emilia.

As to the second query, the short answer is that not all balsamic is created traditionally. But to understand the differences, let's contextualize this famed food craft.

The first written testimonials to the quality of the vinegar from the area dates back to 1046, but it is only in 1747 that the term balsamic appears next to the word vinegar to designate the best of Modena's Palazzo Ducale production. By then, this rare condiment was coveted by courtiers all over Europe looking to ingratiate themselves with their kings and queens.

Balsamic making remained within and for the personal use of the area's noble and upper-middle-class families until the late nineteenth century, when increased access to trade created a market demand that outgrew the supply. Eventually, the opportunity for lucre was seized, and competitively priced condiments with the phrase balsamic vinegar in their name found their way onto market shelves.

As the terms lost their distinguishing connotation, craftspeople dedicated to quality and transparency banded together to protect the work and traditions of centuries. Today, balsamic vinegar producers from Modena and Reggio Emilia answer to outside organizations that uphold strict production standards and have consortia that safeguard them against counterfeiting.

The two provinces produce three vinegars that are sanctioned by the European Union: *aceto balsamico tradizionale di Modena PDO, aceto balsamico tradizionale di Reggio Emilia PDO,* and *aceto balsamico di Modena PGI.*

The two traditional vinegars are made with nothing but the cooked grape must from varietals autochthonous to and grown in their respective territories. After cooking and fermenting, they age for a minimum of twelve years, during which the vinegar lives in an unsealed series of barrels of decreasing size, known as the batteria, in well-aired attics where it can fully benefit from seasonal weather patterns. The vinegar naturally reduces via evaporation, and once a year, it undergoes *travaso e rincalzo,* a technique that involves pouring some of the vinegar from one barrel into the next barrel down to top it up, starting at the second to the smallest barrel. Each stage of production is subject to controls.

Once aging is complete, the vinegar is blindly evaluated by independent panels and, provided it passes muster, sent to bottling facilities that pack it in specific 100cc bottles: a pot-bellied flask with a long neck for Modena and an upside-down tulip for Reggio Emilia. Each bottle is sealed and imprinted with a unique traceable code and then sent back to the producer.

The producer affixes labels with the provenance, PDO seal, and aging. Modena classifies its traditional balsamic as *tradizionale*, at least twelve years old and *tradizionale extravecchio*, twenty-five or older. Reggio Emilia uses colors: *aragosta* (lobster) and *argento* (silver) are both at least twelve years old with some distinct characteristics, and *oro* (gold) is twenty-five or older.

Mariangela Montanari of Acetaia La Cà dal Nôn in Vignola, in the province of Modena, one of a handful of female traditional balsamic makers, says: "Cooked grapes must start sweet and slowly acquires acidity during the acetic fermentation, all the while maintaining the softness derived from the initial cooking. Aging imparts depth, structure, and complexity. The result is a soft, wide acidity." (Author's note: Acidity is "wide" when it doesn't pinch the throat but instead engages the whole oral and nasal cavity without causing the lips to pucker and the nose to twitch.)

To get to the finish line, the human factor is critical at every step. From careful prime-ingredient sourcing to monitoring the cooking of the must and creating synergy between the year's harvest and the fermentation environment, the craftsperson is the determining element for excellence.

Balsamico di Modena PGI has a shorter pedigree than its traditional forebears and is produced in both Modena and Reggio Emilia. It is a simplified product answering market demand by trying to reproduce some of the prized traits of traditional PDO balsamic vinegars.

The PGI vinegar is a blend of at least 20 percent of cooked or concentrated grape must, at least 10 percent red wine vinegar, and a percentage of balsamic vinegar PGI aged for at least ten years. Up to 2 percent caramel is allowed to aid color and viscosity. The grape varietals, while specific, do not have to be locally grown. The final product ages for sixty days. If it goes over three years, it can be called *invecchiato* (aged). Easy raw material sourcing and short aging make it much more affordable. A 500cc bottle may cost as little as eight dollars and will rarely go above fifty dollars.

The bottles vary in size and shape and may be made of glass, wood, or terra-cotta. The label must read aceto balsamico di Modena PGI and bear the PGI blue-and-yellow dot. The spectrum of ingredient percentages yields a wide array of profiles, from the angularly sharp to the rotundly sweet.

In the kitchen, PDO and PGI balsamics cohabit civilly with different roles. PDO vinegars are hardly ever cooked and should be used sparingly. They sublimate bites of parmigiano reggiano and are fantastic in cocktails. Drizzle them over dairy or fat-rich dishes, steamed vegetables, and even fish. Two or three drops will change a sauce and push a custard from competent to unforgettable.

PGI balsamic finds space between the softly acidic notes of a PDO traditional balsamic and the sharp tang of red wine vinegar. It is good for salad dressing, a sweet-and-sour preparation, and a marinade. It also withstands heat well and can be used to make a reduction or deepen the flavor of a braise.

With the exception of the custard, which calls for a Modena balsamic vinegar PGI, all recipes in this chapter use traditional balsamic vinegar PDO. You can find a list of sources at the end of the book.

Finally, when it comes to the many other balsamic products, the majority are nothing more than vinegar with some added sweetener. But there is a small group that demands attention. Current generations of traditional balsamic vinegar makers, such as Mariangela Montanari of Acetaia La Cà dal Nôn, and Andrea Bezzecchi of Acetaia San Giacomo, are developing younger condiments rooted in the tradition of creating acidity by simply acetifying cooked grape must. These products are aged for relatively short periods and have their own new and original version of sweet-and-sour. They are proof that the Italian tradition of quality can be maintained even while it evolves in step with the times.

Mixologists have yet to discover that the sweet-and-sour tones of traditional balsamic make the vinegar an ideal cocktail ingredient. For years, I have been mixing extravecchio with tap water, gin, and everything in between. This recipe is a good starter cocktail. Once you get the taste of what traditional balsamic can do as a mixer, spin your imagination into trial and success. When it comes to traditional balsamic, there is no error.

I prefer a twenty-five-year-plus vinegar for this cocktail, but a younger traditional balsamic will work. Choose strawberries that are barely on the ripe side of rotten; their sweetness is a suited mate to balsamic. You can also carry this drink through the seasons. Make it winter festive with pomegranate seeds, opt for pear in fall, and use cherries in spring.

Prosecco alle fragole e aceto balsamico tradizionale
Prosecco cocktail with traditional balsamic vinegar and strawberries

FOR 4 PEOPLE WITH REFILLS

8 overripe small strawberries (or 4 larger berries)

2 tablespoons traditional balsamic vinegar

1 bottle / 750 ml chilled Prosecco

Wash the strawberries without hulling them. If using large berries, halve them.

Line up four champagne flutes. Pour the vinegar to a depth ⅛ inch / 3 mm—about ¾ teaspoon—into the bottom of each glass. Add a spoon of Prosecco and mix gently to temper the viscosity of the balsamic, allowing the vinegar to disperse more evenly.

Slowly slide in more Prosecco from the side of each flute, filling to within about 1 inch / 2.5 cm of the rim.

Gently squeeze the strawberries between your fingers to bruise them slightly and release some sugary juice. Drop a strawberry into each flute.

Serve the cocktails while still cold and refill when the time comes.

I am a consistent credit giver to those who inspire my cooking, but this is one recipe for which I wish I could take all the glory. Alas, I cannot: it spun out of the fervid culinary imagination of my favorite balsamic vinegar producer and darling friend, Mariangela Montanari, whose lively home has become a mandatory stop on all my visits to Italy.

Lardo is becoming easier to source, but if you cannot find it, a paper-thin slice of pancetta is a good stand-in. While caper leaves (see page 60) might seem an extravagance, I know you will soon depend on their fleshy zing. Should you nonetheless opt to live life without them, you can finish the dish with a few salt-packed capers, well rinsed, and soaked in warm water while the pears are baking.

Pere al forno con lardo sciolto, nocciole e aceto balsamico tradizionale
Roasted pears with melted lardo, hazelnuts, and traditional balsamic vinegar

Heat the oven to 375°F / 190°C / gas mark 5.

Peel the pears and halve them lengthwise. Scoop out the core. Slice each half across from stem to base in slices ⅛ inch / 3 mm thick, keeping them together—think Hasselback potato.

Arrange each pear half in an individual baking dish. Cut the lemon in half and sprinkle a few drops of juice on the pear halves. Place the dishes on a sheet pan and bake the pears for about 25 to 30 minutes, until they are tender enough to be pierced with ease but not jammy.

Remove from the oven and immediately drape a lardo slice over each pear half. Dot with the vinegar, dust with the hazelnuts, and finish with the caper leaves. Serve warm.

FOR 4 PEOPLE

2 ripe but firm pears

1 Meyer lemon

4 paper-thin slices lardo (the length of the pears)

Traditional balsamic vinegar extravecchio, for finishing

2 tablespoons chopped toasted hazelnuts

4 caper leaves

Think of this risotto as a cheat version of the classic risotto alla milanese con ossobuco—all the pleasure without the hassle of braising meat for over an hour. But the balsamic is what pushes this dish from satisfying to unforgettable. Its pucker plays in tune with both the sweetness of the saffron and unctuousness of the marrow, leaving your mouth coated in long-lasting flavor balance.

Risotto al midollo di bue, zafferano e aceto balsamico tradizionale

Risotto with bone marrow, saffron, and traditional balsamic vinegar

FOR 4 PEOPLE

5 full marrowbones

Salt and pepper

1 teaspoon saffron threads

1 small shallot

2 tablespoons unsalted butter

1 cup / 200 g rice for risotto

1 cup / 240 ml dry white wine

¼ cup / 5 g loosely packed parsley leaves

½ cup / 120 ml grated parmigiano reggiano

Traditional balsamic vinegar, for finishing

Heat the broiler. Place the marrowbones on a sheet pan and season on both sides with salt and pepper. Slide the pan under the broiler and leave until the marrow is bubbly and melted all the way through. It should take 10 to 13 minutes, depending on the size of the bones and the quantity of marrow.

In the meantime, pour 5 cups / 1.2 L water into a saucepan, season it with 2 teaspoons salt, and place it over medium-high heat. As soon as it comes to a boil, add half of the saffron threads, cover it, and leave it over the lowest heat to keep it from evaporating.

Grate the shallot on the second smallest holes of a box grater.

Drop the butter into a wide saucepan or sauté pan no more than 4 inches / 10 cm deep over medium-low heat. When the butter is completely melted and beginning to foam, add the shallot and sauté, stirring occasionally, until it is glassy, hazy, and fragrant. It will take 3 to 4 minutes.

Stir the rice into the butter and shallot and raise the heat to medium. Set a timer for 20 minutes.

continued

Stir the rice to coat it in deliciousness for 1 to 2 minutes, until it is shiny and translucent and has lost its dusty smell. Raise the heat to high and pour in the wine. When the wine no longer smells acidic and caresses rather than curls your nose, add 4 cups / 950 ml of the hot saffron-flavored salted water. It will come to a boil almost immediately. Lower the heat until the rice is at a lively bubble but not boiling. You will need to stay close to the stove, but there will be no need to stir; just move the rice occasionally to check that it isn't sticking.

Prepare the garnishes. Mince the parsley. Heat a small frying pan over medium heat until hovering your hand over it feels uncomfortable. Toss in the remaining saffron threads and turn off the heat. Swirl the saffron around the hot pan to make its fragrance bloom, then crumble it between your fingertips.

At minute 10, the rice grains will have grown considerably but still be completely covered in the liquid, which will be cloudy but still quite soupy.

The marrowbones should be ready by now. Scoop the marrow of the fullest bone into a small bowl and cover the rest of the bones with aluminum foil to keep warm.

At about minute 15, taste the rice for salt and adjust as necessary. The liquid will be detectably starchy, and the rice will be close to the surface but barely visible. If the tips of the rice grains are peeking above the surface of the liquid, add a ladleful of the hot saffron water.

At minute 18, the rice should be easily visible above the surface and the liquid tightening but still a little runny. If it is too dense, add a little more hot saffron water. Stay close, wooden spoon in hand.

By minute 20, the rice should be fully visible; the grains will be together but separate and easily move around when the pan is twirled.

Turn off the heat and vigorously stir in 2 tablespoons of the cheese and the marrow scooped out of the large bone. Season the risotto with pepper to suit your taste and divide it among four warm dinner plates. Place a marrowbone on each plate. Dust with the parsley and garnish with the crumbled saffron. Drizzle with the balsamic. Serve right away with the remaining cheese and the balsamic bottle on the side.

I have been making this pasta for twenty-plus years, and I think of it as a seminal expression of the evolution of my relationship with traditional balsamic vinegar. I had always considered it a special occasion ingredient, a flavor to share with a chosen few who could understand its depths, until I saw someone I considered very in the know nonchalantly dripping it on roasted vegetables first, then over just-out-of-the-refrigerator spreadable cheese, and, to end, on vanilla ice cream. The apparent mundaneness of these pairings reframed traditional balsamic with an everyday-hero quality I had failed to see.

This is a dish best made in late spring to early summer when spring onions abound and Gadzukes zucchini—those grooved, dense-fleshed, striated squashes that look like asterisks when sliced crosswise—are in season. But other zucchini will work, or even yellow squash, as long as you choose small, taut, and compact specimens. And if you cannot find spring onions, use a small shallot or 2 scallions.

Gemelli alle zucchine, ricotta salata e aceto balsamico tradizionale
Gemelli with zucchini, ricotta salata, and traditional balsamic vinegar

Fill a pot with 3 quarts / 3 L water, cover it, and set it over heat to come to a boil.

While the water heats, cut the zucchini lengthwise into 4 wedges, then thinly slice each quarter crosswise. Cut the onion in half from stem to root and slice into paper-thin half-moons. Pick the mint leaves from the stems, stack them, roll them up tightly lengthwise, and slice them crosswise into thin ribbons.

Pour enough olive oil into a 12-inch / 30-cm frying pan to lightly coat its bottom. Set the pan over medium-low heat and warm until the fragrance of the oil reaches your nostrils without you having to bend over the stove. Add the onion, half of the mint, and 1 teaspoon salt and cook, stirring occasionally, until the onion has surrendered its stiffness and looks glassy and hazy. It will take 6 to 8 minutes.

FOR 6 PEOPLE

3 small, tender zucchini

1 spring onion

2 mint sprigs

Extra-virgin olive oil as needed

Salt and pepper

1 package (1 pound / 450 g) gemelli (or other short pasta)

½ cup / 60 g shredded ricotta salata

Traditional balsamic vinegar, for finishing

continued

Gemelli alle zucchine, ricotta salata e aceto balsamico tradizionale, continued

The water should be boiling by now. Season it with 1 tablespoon salt, stir in the pasta, and cover the pot. Set a timer for 2 minutes shy of the suggested cooking time. When the water starts to boil again, remove the cover and adjust the heat so the water is at a lively, but not rolling, boil.

Add the zucchini to the frying pan and raise the heat to medium. Cook, stirring often, for 8 to 12 minutes, until the zucchini are tender but still soulful and bright green with sporadic spots of caramelization. If it is necessary to prevent the zucchini from sticking and burning, add dribbles of warm water. Sample the zucchini, season them with salt and pepper to suit your taste, and transfer to a warm serving bowl.

The pasta should be cooked by now. Lift it out of the pot with a handheld strainer and transfer it to the bowl with the zucchini. Add 3 to 4 tablespoons of the pasta cooking water, and 3 tablespoons of the ricotta salata, then toss until the starch and fat bind into a creamy gossamer around the pasta. Stir in 1 to 2 tablespoons of olive oil to make the dish sheen. Toss thoroughly.

Drip 10 to 12 drops of the balsamic onto the pasta and toss again. Artfully drizzle with a few more drops of vinegar and garnish with the remaining mint. For maximum happiness, serve right away, accompanied by the remaining ricotta salata and the balsamic bottle.

I grew up understanding that one should appreciate as many parts of an animal as possible. It is a sustainable way of eating that is also compassionate toward the animal whose life was meant for our nourishment. Offal was always a part of our family diet.

Liver is the most commonly available offal. It is tasty, easy to cook, inexpensive, and good for you. Indeed, this recipe lifted my low-iron-related waning energy level during pregnancy and during perimenopause, which is like pregnancy except much longer and without the glowing skin, lustrous locks, and happy ending. All jesting aside, give liver a shot. If you still don't like it, swap it for thin cutlets of your favorite meat.

I like all kinds of liver, but for this dish, I recommend rose-colored calf's liver. If you cannot find it, delicate chicken livers will also work.

Fegato di vitello al burro all'aceto balsamico tradizionale
Butter-panfried calf's liver with traditional balsamic vinegar

Rinse the liver and pat it dry with paper towels. Season each liver slice all over with salt, then dredge it lightly in the flour on both sides. Shake off the excess flour until the liver appears to be wearing a thin veil.

Heat the olive oil in a frying pan over medium heat until it shimmers and its fragrance effortlessly wafts to your nostrils. Add 2 tablespoons of the butter. When it has melted into a foam and taken on a light beige color, lay the liver slices in the pan. Listen for a gentle, low sizzle. The liver will cook quite quickly; 3 to 5 minutes per side, depending on the thickness of the slices.

Brown the liver lightly until you can easily lift it and turn it over. Now brown the other side and cook until the liver is still tender and releases a tinge of pink when pricked. Lift the meat from the pan and arrange it on a warm platter. Cover with aluminum foil so the heat doesn't disperse.

Raise the heat to high and add ½ cup / 120 ml warm water to the pan, then scrape the caramelized bits from the pan bottom. When the water boils, plop in the remaining 1 tablespoon butter and stir continuously to emulsify. Taste and season with salt to suit your palate.

Douse the pan with the vinegar and turn off the heat almost right away. The sauce should cook no further. Swirl the pan to meld the flavors, then stir well. Pour the sauce over the liver slices, top with a few grinds of white pepper, dust with the parsley, and serve right away.

FOR 4 PEOPLE

4 calf's liver slices, each 4 ounces / 115 g

Salt and white pepper

2 tablespoons all-purpose flour (for gluten-free, use cornstarch)

2 tablespoons extra-virgin olive oil

3 tablespoons unsalted butter

2 tablespoons traditional balsamic vinegar

1 small handful parsley leaves, minced

This cheat on crème caramel is embarrassingly fast to put together. It's not as glossy and relatively smooth but it can hold its own at the end of any meal. I prefer to make individual servings as they cook more quickly, but you can also bake the custard in one big mold.

Crema cotta con riduzione di aceto balsamico
Baked custard with balsamic vinegar reduction

FOR 6 PEOPLE

1 cup / 240 ml Modena balsamic vinegar

2 tablespoons natural cane sugar

3 eggs

1 egg yolk

1 ¼ cups / 300 ml heavy cream or whole milk

⅓ cup / 70 g granulated sugar if using cream, or 4½ tablespoons / 60 g granulated sugar if using milk

Heat the oven to 325°F / 165°C / gas mark 3. Prepare a 6-cup muffin pan.

Stir together the vinegar and cane sugar in a small saucepan and set over medium heat. Reduce the mixture at a low boil for 10 to 15 minutes.

Whisk the eggs, egg yolk, cream, and granulated sugar in a bowl with glee until the mixture is uniformly yellow, has puffed slightly, and the sugar has melted. To check this, dip your thumb and index finger into the mixture then rub them together; if you perceive grit, whisk some more.

Coat the bottom of each muffin cup with 1 generous tablespoon of the vinegar reduction. Divide the egg mixture evenly among the muffin cups.

Select a roasting or baking pan large enough to accommodate the muffin pan. Place a small cooling rack in the roasting pan and set the muffin pan on the rack. Pour in water two-thirds of the way up the sides of the muffin cups.

Tent the roasting pan loosely with aluminum foil and carefully slide it into the oven. Bake for about 40 minutes, until the custards are just slightly tremulous and have a taut, puffy film keeping them securely encased.

Remove the roasting pan from the oven and let the muffin pan cool in the water before serving. Note that it is normal for the custards to deflate.

When you are ready to plate the custards, run a knife around the edge of each muffin cup and gently shake the pan to loosen them. Line a sheet pan with parchment paper and turn it upside down over the muffin pan to seal it. Hold the two pans tightly together and invert them in a quick, swift motion. Do not hesitate or the custards will feel your fear. Tap the bottom of each muffin cup lightly with a spoon or the handle of a dinner knife, then gently shake the two sandwiched pans. Give the custards a moment to release onto the parchment, then carefully peel off the muffin pan.

Plate the custards on frilly, lovely plates to distract the eater from the fact that they are kind of ugly, then serve.

CHAPTER 2

CONSERVE DI POMODORO / CONSERVED TOMATOES

The all-season character actor of the Italian pantry theater

I pelati ci sono? (Do we have peeled tomatoes?) If the answer to that question is no, then it's time for the weekly shopping. No Italian household can peacefully exist knowing that there are no conserved tomatoes in its pantry. The love affair between Italians and tomatoes, however torrid and intense, is relatively recent, as the seeds of this fruit indigenous to the Americas did not land on Italian soil until the end of the sixteenth century. The golden fruit—*pomo d'oro* and later *pomodoro*—found agricultural sublimation in the south, particularly in the region of Campania. But within a century, *pomodori* gained a place of honor that cannot be prescinded from the cooking of the whole Italian peninsula. That place of honor includes preserving them.

As any good Italian, I have an unbridled love for tomatoes. When they are in season, I eat them virtually every day. For the rest of the year, my pantry has a jealously guarded shelf dedicated to all manner of conserved tomatoes.

Pelati—whole peeled tomatoes—are the most common and versatile form and by far my favorite. Any type of tomato can be canned into *pelati*, either in water or its own juice, but some are more suited than others. Long, thin-skinned, dense-fleshed San Marzano tomatoes are sweet and with few seeds, and they are the top pick for canning. The San Marzano from the Agro Sarnese-Nocerino region, in the province of Salerno in Campania, is considered the best of this variety and carries the EU red-and-gold seal of PDO products.

Neapolitan *pacchetella* is the filet mignon of *pelati*. San Marzanos at peak maturity are skinned, quartered, and seeded, then packed upright in jars. *Pacchetella* barely touches the pan and already the fragrance of the sun that's been kissing those tomatoes all summer fills the kitchen. This should be the choice for anyone trying to recreate that unforgettable bowl of spaghetti al pomodoro from their Italian trip.

Polpa di pomodoro—"tomato pulp"—is tomatoes that have been skinned, crushed, and drained. *Polpa* is thick and chunky, and because it cooks quickly with results comparable to *pelati*, it has gained a steady spot in Italian pantries. I use it to make fast one-pot meals in which the protein needs to cook quickly to achieve the right consistency.

Passata is the third most popular tomato craft. *Passare* is the Italian word for both milling and straining. Indeed, to become *passata*, tomatoes are milled and then strained of their skins and seeds into a smooth, runny sauce that is thickened over heat before bottling. Because it's already cooked, it needs just heating and seasoning, and it's good for sauces, soups, stews, and on pizza.

Milled and strained tomatoes can be further cooked to extract their essence into *concentrato* (concentrate) or into the Sicilian *estratto* (extract). Concentrato—akin to paste—is packed in tubes and comes in regular, double, or triple thickness, according to how much the tomato puree was reduced. The king is *estratto*. This Sicilian pantry staple is made by a combination of cooking and sun-drying tomatoes. Its red is deep enough to be brown, and its consistency is that of modeling clay. These three wonder ingredients can correct or deepen the character of a dish without revealing their presence. For example, when a tomato sauce is too sharp, a small spoonful of double concentrate and a pinch of salt will set it on course. Want to push roast beef pan sauce over the top? Just add ¼ teaspoon *estratto*.

Sun-dried tomatoes, long a local specialty of southern Italian regions, crept into chefs' kitchens in the 1980s and have since moved to the mainstream. Packed in oil, they are flavorful appetizers and can complement a salad or sandwich. When dry-packed, they are a chewy and healthy snack. Reconstituted, they make a punchy sauce. When purchasing sun-dried tomatoes, keep in mind that the brighter their red, the more likely they are to have been treated with sulfites to maintain color.

Many Italians can their own tomatoes. This family tradition has been pivotal in preserving heirloom seed. Moreover, farming communities are riding the current focus on biodiversity, and having shored up the support of nonprofit and governmental organizations, they have mobilized to carve the market space heirloom tomatoes need to thrive. Jars of these special crops are available everywhere. Piennolo del Vesuvio and Corbarino—varieties of small tomato grown on the mountain slopes of Campania—are two examples. Their secret is the whiff of salt they absorb from exposure to sea breezes. They are so good that they can be blitzed into gazpacho straight out of the jar, and they are the top choice for quick-cooking seafood dishes.

In late summer, when the Grand Prix circuit lulls and before soccer season starts again, families all over Italy engage in the sport of *fare i pomodori*, or "put up sauce," as I have heard many Americans of Italian descent refer to the activity. The task can consume a weekend or a few weeks, depending on the number of participants, the preferred method, and if the tomatoes come from a family patch that continues to produce or are bought at the market. In my childhood home, there was plenty of help. We had tomatoes from our own vegetable garden and gifts from friends and neighbors. My mother made *passata*, and she entrusted *pelati* to Alberta, my dad's housekeeper. My allegiance was always to Alberta's *pelati*. To this day, hers are the secrets I bring to my own *fare i pomodori*. The only change to Alberta's method is the addition of lemon juice. This enhanced safety technique raises acidity without compromising the end result, and it was taught to me by my friend and master preserver, Shakirah Simley.

Pomodori in vaso
Jarred tomatoes

Fill your two largest pots two-thirds full with water and place them over high heat to come to a boil.

Turn the oven on to the lowest setting. Wash the jars in very hot water, dry them, and line them up on a sheet pan. Slide the pan into the oven. Wash and dry the lids well and keep them in a clean bowl.

Rinse the tomatoes and use the tip of a paring knife to score an X on the butt end of each one. The incision should be barely skin-deep.

Line up two large bowls. Fill the one closest to the stove halfway with ice and then submerge the ice in water. Leave the other bowl empty.

The water should be boiling by now. Drop as many tomatoes as will fit comfortably into each pot without the water overflowing. Boil the tomatoes for 1 to 2 minutes, until their skins are lifting and retracting at the Xs. Lift them out with a handheld strainer and plunge them into the ice bath. The shock will cause the skins to come off easily. Peel each tomato and put it into the empty bowl. Process all the tomatoes, topping up the bowl with ice as the hot tomatoes melt the ice.

continued

FOR TWELVE 1-PINT / 475-ML CANNING JARS

15 pounds / 6.8 kg San Marzano or other suitable canning tomatoes

36 basil leaves (optional)

⅓ cup / 80 ml strained lemon juice

Remove the jars from the oven and pack them with the tomatoes, leaving ¼-inch / 6-mm headspace. Tap each jar on the counter to remove any air bubbles. If there are stubborn bubbles, use clean chopsticks to redistribute the tomatoes and eliminate empty pockets.

Push 3 basil leaves into each jar and then sprinkle with 1½ teaspoons lemon juice. Wipe and dry the edges of the rims of the jars with a clean cloth and screw on the lids until fingertip tight.

Lower the filled jars into a water bath canner or into a large pot with a lid and a cooling rack on the bottom. Fill the pot with enough water to cover the jars by 2 inches / 5 cm. Turn the heat to high and process the jarred tomatoes for 10 minutes from the time the water comes to a boil. Turn off the heat and remove the jars from the water without tilting them. Place them upright on the counter and let cool undisturbed for 12 hours.

Press the center of each jar lid with a finger; it shouldn't move. If it clicks up and down, the jar isn't properly sealed. Refrigerate any unsealed tomato jars and use them within 2 weeks at most. All safely sealed jars can be stored in the pantry for up to 2 years.

There are as many meat sauces as there are mothers in Italy, and we each have our own secrets. Allow me to unveil mine. Pancetta is essential, but I cream it instead of chopping it, as braised whole bites of even the best fat can unpleasantly coat the roof of your mouth. Use tomato concentrate or paste instead of canned tomatoes. And most importantly, ignore the grating wormwood of inadequacy caused by those who boast about hours of cooking. Spare yourself that exercise in futility; follow my recipe instead and join the ranks of seasoned cooks already converted to my version of ragù alla bolognese.

Ragù della maestra
Teacher's bolognese

Cut the pancetta into chunks and run it through a food processor until it is creamy. Transfer it to a large bowl and add the beef and 2 teaspoons salt. Massage the mixture to blend the ingredients evenly. Leave on the counter to come to room temperature while you prepare the rest of the ingredients.

To make the aromatic soffritto base, peel and cut the carrots, onion, and celery into ⅛-inch / 3-mm dice. Heat a wide, shallow, heavy-bottomed saucepan over medium heat until hovering a hand over the pan feels slightly uncomfortable. Pour in the olive oil. When the oil looks shimmery and its fragrance wafts to your nose, add the butter. In about 1 minute, when the butter foams and turns imperceptibly beige, add the diced vegetables, bay leaves, and 1 teaspoon salt. Stir with a wooden spoon for 3 to 4 minutes, until the vegetables glisten. Lower the heat to medium-low and cover the pan.

The vegetables will gradually release their moisture and fragrance. They will emit a slow and full sizzle. As the moisture cooks off, the sizzle will get tighter and crinkly. Keep your ears pricked: if the sizzle becomes a screech, the vegetables are calling for help. Add 2 to 3 tablespoons warm water so they do not stick and burn and then continue cooking. Eventually, they will be golden hued and fork-tender, smell sweet, look creamy, and feel yielding.

MAKES 4 CUPS / 950 ML

4-ounce / 115-g piece pancetta

1½ pounds / 680 g ground beef

Salt and pepper

2 carrots

1 medium yellow onion

1 celery rib

2 tablespoons olive oil

2 tablespoons unsalted butter

2 bay leaves

2 cups / 475 ml beef stock

2 tablespoons tomato concentrate (or paste)

1 cup / 240 ml dry red wine

1 cup / 240 ml whole milk

continued

This stage will take 30 to 40 minutes; do not rush it. A well-tended and developed soffritto makes the difference between a solid bolognese and one so good you dream of it when enjoying your morning coffee. Uncover the pan and make sure the excess moisture has evaporated before moving to the next step.

Heat the stock on the stove or in the microwave and dilute the tomato concentrate in it. Cover it so it stays hot until you use it.

Raise the heat to high under the vegetables and add the ground meat–pancetta mixture. Stir almost continuously and break down the clumps as small as they can get before your patience is tried. A wooden spoon will do the job, but a potato masher is the most apt tool.

In about 5 minutes, the meat will change color from a deep rose to a grayish beige. Douse it with the wine, then scrape all the caramelized bits off the bottom of the pan. Stand by the stove and when the scent of the wine no longer punches your face and instead caresses your nose sweetly, stir in the stock-tomato mixture. When the sauce comes to a boil, reduce the heat to medium-low, cover the pan, and let the meat simmer for 45 minutes. Remove the lid and raise the heat to medium-high so the last of the moisture can evaporate.

Heat the milk in a measuring pitcher in the microwave until is just below boiling; the timing will depend on your microwave. Reduce the heat to low under the meat and slowly stream the milk into the meat sauce while stirring continuously. Let simmer gently for an additional 10 to 15 minutes, until the milk has evaporated. Stir in a generous pinch of pepper, then taste the sauce and adjust salt and pepper to suit your palate.

At this point, the ragù is ready to dress pasta or refrigerate for later use. But if you want to make the meat clumps smaller, pulse it with a handheld blender six to eight times, dipping it into a different area of the sauce each time.

The ragù can safely live in the refrigerator for about a week, or it can be frozen for up to 3 months. The most suited pasta shapes for it are tagliatelle and rigatoni, but any other shapes you might have on hand will do.

For best dressing results, heat the sauce in a large sauté pan. Cook the pasta in boiling salted water for 2 minutes shy of the suggested cooking time. Lift it out of the pot with a handheld strainer, transfer it to the ragù, add ½ cup / 120 ml of the pasta cooking water, then swirl and jostle the pan over high heat until the water retreats onto the pasta surface in a gossamer of fat and starch. Dust with grated parmigiano reggiano and serve right away.

Years ago, when the head count for an event I was catering unexpectedly grew so close to the start time that I didn't have time to shop, I scuba dove to the bottom of my refrigerator and through the recesses of my pantry and emerged with this soup. It was the course attendees inquired about the most that evening, and it has become the anecdote to best illustrate how successful the marriage of ingenuity and good ingredients can be. Store this soup right back into the bottles of the *passata* you use to make it. Since there is no animal fat, it will keep refrigerated for up to 2 weeks, or you can freeze it for up to 6 months. To make it more filling, serve it with croutons. To personalize it, use a different herb or spice it with red chili flakes.

Vellutata di pomodoro, carote e porri al profumo di arancio e zenzero
Orange and ginger–scented tomato, carrots, and leek cream

MAKES 1 ½ QUARTS / 1.5 L

3 leeks

4 carrots

1-inch / 2.5-cm piece ginger

1 orange

6 chives

4 tablespoons / 60 ml extra-virgin olive oil, plus more for finishing

Salt and pepper

4 cups / 950 ml tomato passata

Strip off the outer layer of each leek, then cut off the root end and the top half of the green part. Cut the leeks in half lengthwise, then thinly slice them crosswise and leave them to soak in a salad spinner filled with water, agitating them periodically to loosen any dirt.

Peel the carrots, halve lengthwise, and then slice them crosswise into thin half-moons. Grate the ginger. Grate 1 teaspoon zest from the orange, then cut the orange in half and juice it. Slice the chives into thin rings. Drain the leeks and shake off the excess water.

Pour 2 tablespoons of the olive oil into a saucepan and place over medium heat until you detect the fragrance of the oil without bending over the stove. Swirl in the ginger and orange zest and season with 1 teaspoon salt. You will smell their intensity in barely a minute; raise the heat all the way up and add the carrots and leeks. Stir to coat in yumminess, then turn down the heat to medium and sweat the vegetables until the leeks are translucent and the carrots begin to yield. This should take about 10 minutes.

Stir in the orange juice and ½ cup / 120 ml water, season with a pinch each of salt and pepper, and partially cover. Cook for about 20 minutes, until the carrots are quite tender and the leeks are soft and look like milk glass. Check periodically to make sure the vegetables aren't sticking to the pan.

Turn up the heat, add the passata, and bring to a boil. Lower the heat to a simmer and sample the soup. Adjust salt and pepper to suit your palate, then cook for another 15 minutes.

Let cool for a couple of minutes, then transfer to a blender and puree until smooth while streaming in the remaining 2 tablespoons olive oil. Taste one last time to adjust salt and pepper as it best suits your palate.

Pour the soup into a tureen or ladle it into individual bowls. Serve warm, garnished with the chives and finished with a few drops of olive oil.

From the 2012 marriage of my friend Antonella on the island of Salina, I still carry so many sensations. The flavors in this recipe are some of them—a few traditionally Sicilian ingredients melded into an innovative dish. The restaurant was Alfredo in Cucina, on a jut of land called Lingua. The bride quelled my excitement by introducing me to the chef from whose very vague guidance I culled this recipe. Pistachio peeling is tedious work, but it does give a cleaner taste. Still, skip it if you are short on time or patience.

Paccheri con ragù di calamari, pomodorini del Piennolo e pistacchi
Paccheri with calamari, Piennolo tomatoes, and pistachio

Heat the oven to 300°F / 150°C / gas mark 2. Drain the tomatoes well, spread them on a sheet pan, and sprinkle with 1 teaspoon salt. Slide the pan into the oven to roast while you prepare the rest of the ingredients.

Cleaning calamari is a messily relaxing business that you will want to carry out in the kitchen sink. Have three small bowls ready: one for the bodies, one for the tentacles, and the third one for the calamari refuse. Place the calamari in a colander and rinse them well. Separate the bodies from the tentacles.

To clean the bodies, dig through the inside of a body to find the feather-shaped bone and pull it all out. If the bone is not the length of the body and tapered on both ends, dive back in for the rest. Hold the calamari by the tip with one hand and run a thumb and index finger along the outside from the tip to the opening to squeeze out the gunk and guts. Repeat until all the bodies are clean.

Pick up a set of tentacles and flip it over; it will look like a bunch of flowers. You will see an opening in the center where a beak-like set of teeth is lodged. Squeeze the opening to pop it out. Turn the tentacles back over and rip any lingering gut-adjacent remnants off the top. Lastly, carefully poke a little tear on each eye with the tip of a paring knife and coax out the tiny, round crystals. Repeat with the remaining tentacles.

Return the calamari bodies and tentacles to the colander for one last quick rinse and leave them to drain while you finish prepping the rest of the ingredients.

continued

FOR 6 PEOPLE

1 jar (18 ounces / 500 g) Piennolo del Vesuvio tomatoes

Salt and pepper

1 pound / 450 g calamari

¼ cup / 30 g raw pistachios

1 zucchini, 3½ to 4½ ounces / 100 to 130 g

½ small yellow or white onion

½ cup / 10 g loosely packed parsley leaves

4 tablespoons / 60 ml extra-virgin olive oil, plus more for finishing

1 cup / 240 ml dry white wine

1 package (1 pound / 450 g) paccheri

Set a small pot of water to boil and ready a small bowl of iced water. Drop the pistachios into the boiling water and leave them for just 1 minute, then fish them out with a tea strainer and immerse them in the ice water. Leave the water at a boil and use it to cook the zucchini for about 10 minutes, until soft enough to pierce with a knife but still bright, then drain. In the meantime, patiently slide the skins off the pistachios.

Mince the onion into a paste. Finely chop the parsley.

Pour 2 tablespoons of the olive oil into a frying pan and set over medium-low heat until the fragrance of the oil wafts to your nostrils without you having to bend over the stove. Add the onion, half of the parsley, and 1 teaspoon salt. Cook, stirring occasionally, for 4 to 5 minutes, until the onion is translucent and hazy.

Fill a pot with 3 quarts / 3 L water, cover it, and set it over heat to come to a boil.

Add the calamari to the pan with the onion and parsley and raise the heat to high. Sauté until their color changes to pink. Douse with the wine. When the acidity of the wine no longer punches your nose and instead its sugariness caresses your eyes, add ¼ cup / 60 ml warm water, cover, and reduce the heat to low.

Braise the seafood for 15 to 25 minutes, until tender. The exact timing will depend on the size of the calamari. Check periodically to make sure some liquid remains on the bottom of the pan. For longer cooking times, you may need to add small amounts of water from time to time.

While the calamari are cooking, puree the zucchini in a blender and coarsely chop the pistachios. Mix the zucchini and chopped pistachios in a warm serving bowl, holding back 1 teaspoon of the pistachios for garnishing.

The water should be boiling by now. Season it with 1 tablespoon salt, stir in the pasta, and cover the pot. Set a timer for 1 minute shy of the suggested cooking time. When the water starts to boil again, remove the cover and adjust the heat so the water is at a lively, but not rolling, boil.

When the calamari are ready, pick out a couple of tentacle bundles and set them aside for garnishing. Pour the rest of the calamari and its cooking liquid into a food processor and pulse a few times until the consistency of a meat sauce. If you don't have a food processor, you can chop them with a chef's knife. Add to the bowl with the zucchini and pistachios and keep warm.

The tomatoes should be ready by now. They should have lost most of their liquid and have a few burnt skin tips here and there. Add them to the bowl with the calamari, then pour in the remaining 2 tablespoons olive oil and stir the contents of the bowl to mix well. Sample a spoonful and adjust salt and pepper to suit your taste.

When the timer goes off, fish the pasta out of the water with a handheld strainer, add it to the serving bowl, and toss everything well. Drizzle with a little olive oil, dust with the remaining parsley, and garnish with the saved tentacles and pistachios. Serve right away.

Forget eggs Benedict and redefine brunch with a dish that is as short in difficulty as it is long in flavor. It can be assembled ahead and baked right before being carried to the table. Toasted slices of country bread are soulmates to this casserole, and a bowl of red chili flakes will cull those who like spice.

Uova in forno alla polpa pomodoro con feta, olive e origano
Eggs baked in tomato pulp with feta, olives, and oregano

FOR 2 PEOPLE

2 tablespoons black olives

2 garlic cloves

4 tablespoons / 60 ml extra-virgin olive oil

1 can (14 ounces / 400 g) polpa di pomodoro (tomato pulp)

2 oregano sprigs

Salt and pepper

4 eggs

¼ cup / 30 g crumbled feta

Heat the oven to 350°F / 180°C / gas mark 4.

Thoroughly wash the brine off the olives, then soak them in warm water until ready to use. Smash and peel the garlic cloves.

Pour 2 tablespoons of the olive oil into a small baking dish and add the garlic. Slide the baking dish into the oven and heat for 5 minutes, just enough for the oil to ensnare some of the garlic's fragrance.

Empty the tomato pulp into a bowl and season it with enough salt and pepper to suit your palate. Drain the olives and rub the oregano sprigs between your palms to release their fragrance. Add the olives and oregano to the tomatoes.

Pull the baking dish out of the oven and discard the garlic cloves, then pour the seasoned tomatoes into it. With the back of a spoon, mark the pulp with four divots the size of an egg, being careful not to go all the way through to the bottom of the dish. Break an egg into a ramekin and slide it into one of the divots. Repeat until all the eggs are nestled in divots.

Drizzle the eggs with the remaining 2 tablespoons olive oil and slide the baking dish back into the oven. Bake for 10 to 25 minutes, depending on how set you prefer your eggs.

Remove from the oven, scatter the feta over the eggs, and serve warm.

In my San Francisco kitchen, cod is king. The cold water of the North Pacific is a haven for this flaky fish, whose fat is both good and good for you. This is my favorite cod recipe for the spring. If you are elsewhere in the spring, you can swap out cod for other white, plump fish. In New York, I have used scrod, in Italy, sea bream or sole. Marjoram can take the place of mint, and if you want to give it a spicy chili kick, it will take it well.

Merluzzo in guazzetto di Corbarini, taccole e menta
Cod stewed in Corbarini, sugar snaps, and mint

Slant the blade of your knife until it is almost parallel to the cutting board and use the heel of your hand to gently press the blade down on the garlic clove until you've cracked the skin. Peel the garlic clove and leave it whole.

Stack the mint leaves, roll them up lengthwise, and slice them crosswise into thin ribbons. Snap any stems off the sugar snaps. Drain the tomatoes into a colander. Season the cod generously on both sides with salt and pepper.

Pour 2 tablespoons of olive oil into a sauté pan, add the garlic, and set over medium heat. When you see tiny bubbles around the garlic, turn it to blister the other side. When the oil shimmers and its fragrance wafts up to your nose without you bending over the stove, discard the garlic.

Add the cod skin side down and cook 6 to 8 minutes until it doesn't stick to the pan when you lift it with a fish spatula. Do not force it; it will easily come loose when it is ready. Turn it over and cook 2 to 4 minutes, until it feels firm and reaches an internal temperature just below 130°F / 55°C.

Move the fish to a plate. Add the remaining oil to the pan. Stir in half of the mint and the peas and sauté for 1 minute to coat the peas in flavor. Raise the heat to high, pour in the tomatoes, and lightly mash them with a wooden spoon. Turn the heat to medium and cook for 5 minutes, enough to bring the peas to tenderness, and slightly thicken the sauce. Taste and adjust salt and pepper to your liking.

Return the fish to the pan and spoon the sauce over it. Cover the pan and turn off the heat. Leave it in the pan until the internal temperature is between 130°F / 55°C and 135°F / 57°C, where cod's distinguishing flaky character is at its best.

Garnish with the remaining mint and a few drops of olive oil, then serve. Be amazed by the sweetness of the Corbarini.

FOR 3 TO 4 PEOPLE

1 garlic clove

4 mint sprigs

1 cup / 100 g sugar snap peas

1 jar (18 ounces / 500 g) Corbarino tomatoes (or other good canned cherry tomatoes) packed in water

1 pound / 450 g skin-on cod fillet, in a single piece

Salt and pepper

3 tablespoons extra-virgin olive oil, plus more for finishing

CHAPTER 3

CAPPERI E OLIVE /
CAPERS & OLIVES

Bold pantry flavor in small, unassuming bites

My parents had intended for the uninhabited part of our home to become apartments for their numerous brood. The plan was foiled by the slow-motion crumbling of their marriage, but the abandoned rooms still served their belief in homesteading as a better way of eating. All through our years living there, those rooms warehoused the many provisions my mother crafted through the seasons. I would sneak in to smell, touch, taste something forbidden. Heaps of dry-cured olives are one of the most vivid of those food memories. By shattered windows and under woodworm-eaten beams, I was slowly enthralled by their fragrance, feel, taste, in that all-encompassing sensorial way with which I still experience food. To this day, the whiff of a dish defined by olives takes me back there.

The magic of olives is that they come already armed with two of the main elements of good cooking: salt and fat. Once heated, olives deliver their barely bitter punch to the dish. When cooking with olives, follow these tips: No matter how they are packed, always rinse them; the conserving elements carry flavors that will impact the end result. When buying olives in brine, choose them with the pit. Pitted olives absorb more conserving solution and lose character. Bother to remove the pit if you have the time, or just include a pit cup in the table setting; people will catch the drift.

Many olive varieties can be transformed into table olives, but only a handful are widely available. Once you have honed in on the Italian varieties (because why wouldn't you?), choose among Castelvetrano, Cerignola, Gaeta, and Taggiasca, the four most widely available ones. Let's look at them in geographical order from bottom to top.

Castelvetrano is a medium-size olive from Sicily. Picked green and conserved in brine or cracked and packed in olive oil with herbs, they resist the teeth with a crunch. They taste young and grassy, with a tang of spring fennel, and are best companions for those proteins, like lamb and fatty fish, whose long-lasting layers of flavor benefit from a quick disruption. Beware of Castelvetrano olives that present in too bright a green. They may be poseurs, as the natural color of these olives is a muted green with a hint of dark yellow.

Cerignola is a large olive from the province of Foggia in Puglia. It can be collected young and green or fully ripe and black. In the green stages, the flesh is firm with notes of preserved lemon. Once matured, the flesh becomes slightly mousse-like, while the skin remains taut and acts as a pleasant barrier to the first bite. Cerignola olives are best eaten on their own, though the green can stand in for Castelvetrano in a pinch.

The Golfo di Gaeta—Gulf of Gaeta—is the body of water along which coastal Lazio bows out and cedes to Campania. It is also where Gaeta olives are plucked at full dark ripeness for dry curing or brining. If I had only one choice of olives, this would be it. They are round and sweet but also carry the salinity that blows in the air of sea-adjacent lands. A dry cure is best to bring out the bitter undertones that make them a good match for proteins and vegetables with softer, more yielding characters, like chicken and beets.

The prized Taggiasca lives in Liguria. The physical layout of the region makes it a limited production that is mostly pressed into excellent olive oil. The olive is small and compact, with an almost fifty-fifty pit-to-flesh ratio. Its variegated color is typical of olives picked halfway to full ripeness. Its flavor is round and floral but still punchy. The Taggiasca is very good in salads or with lean fish and is also ideal for long braises, as it maintains its structure during extended exposure to heat.

Lastly, a quick bonus recipe to up your aperitivo game: Rinse and drain the olives, then spice and herb them to your pleasure. Toss them in a frying pan with 1 tablespoon olive oil over the lowest heat setting for about 20 minutes. Serve warm and awaken the crowd to the possibilities of olives.

While I grew up aware of the times and lives of olives, it wasn't until my twenties that I fully contextualized capers, thanks to my friend Adriana Marino. She hails from Naples, married a Sicilian, and settled in Puglia. She is mom to the one other man I got close to marrying, she's the best southern Italian cook I know, and, just as my own mother did, Adriana preserves the seasons. A long-ago early summer on the island of Salina, she took me caper picking and taught me the secrets of *capperi delle isole*—"island capers." Indeed, capers from the Sicilian islands of Salina and Pantelleria, protected respectively by PDO and PGI certifications, are considered the best available. Both islands have caper farms as well as an abundance of wild-growing caper bushes from which locals collect and cure capers for the year.

Caper bushes start with a branchy trunk at the very base covered by numerous thin and flexible branches arching down and bearing rows of alternating heart-shaped leaves. A caper bush can be planted on the ground, but it is at its most beautiful when sprouting like mussed curls from cracks in a wall. These shrubs require dry soil, warmth, and direct sun and have a short span of tolerance for temperatures below 32°F (0°C).

Starting in spring and continuing through late summer, caper bushes spin a cycle of delicacies. First come capers, the buds of the flowers that will eventually break through. Caper flowers are white, four-petaled beauties that bloom through the summer with a central tuft ranging in color from hot pink to psychedelic violet. Eventually, the flower gives way to a fruit, the pointy, long-stemmed, ovate berry we know as the caperberry. Throughout the cycle, leaves of varying sizes are collected and preserved.

Leaves, capers, and caperberries all come in different sizes and several declensions.

A salad of quickly boiled tender caper leaves and potatoes is a specialty of the Sicilian islands. Larger leaves are conserved in oil. They bring an unexpected kick of crunch to a salad and are a treat battered and then deep-fried.

Capers range from four to fourteen millimeters in diameter (scant one-quarter to one-half inch), depending on when they are picked. The earlier, tightly closed buds are the more prized for their strong scent and delicate flavor. As the capers grow and the sepals start separating to let out the flower, the aroma dissipates and the flavor becomes more pungent. The tiniest capers are known as lilliput. They are hard to find and quite pricey. Non-pareil is the next size up. After that, they are grouped into small, medium, and large. Use the larger ones for chopping into roasts or braises or long-cooking sauces. Medium and small are good for salads and quick-cooking sauces or minced into dressings like salsa verde. The two smallest-caliber capers are the ones to keep whole and use as that last-minute flavor spark.

The flower is edible and Italian chefs have begun to include it in their dishes for its beauty and fragrance.

Caperberries—*cucunci* in Italian—are also best picked small, as the seeds become large and woody before the fruit splits. Use them sliced in salads and sandwiches, or whole to cut through the fat of a cheese. With their stem on, they can take the place of olives for an aperitivo. Do keep in mind that capers and caperberries are not interchangeable in cooking.

Both the buds and the fruits start their lives as food crafts in a salt cure at the end of which they are ready as is or they can be packed in olive oil or vinegar. Salt packing best preserves their character. Oil packed can be quite tasty if packed in a good-quality oil. In a vinegar solution, they lose firmness and their defining aroma marries with the tang of vinegar.

However they are packed, capers and caperberries need careful rinsing before use. If using salt packed, rinse them well, then soak them in warm water and still go easy on salting the recipe. Capers can also be sun-dried or dehydrated, then left whole, ground, or pulverized and used as a seasoning.

Out of all that lives in my pantry, capers and caperberries are the most magic. They are good with oil or butter, lemon and orange, meat, fish, pasta, vegetables, and fruits. I have even eaten them candied. In fact, try as I might, I cannot think of anything with which these umami-laden buds and berries do not get along.

My half British—half Egyptian mother-in-law adores my cooking. She and I spend days planning flavors that will become the memories of our times together. As a mostly single mother, she put dinner on the table every night after clocking in a day as a professor at Duke University. I think she would be surprised to learn how much she has informed how I move in the kitchen and has expanded the way I pair flavors. This *tramezzino* is a bow to the fantastic Dr. Elisabeth Fox, inspired by our ploughman's lunches of Cheddar and chutney sandwiches.

Tramezzini con cucunci e cheddar
Caperberries and Cheddar tea sandwiches

FOR 4 TEA SANDWICHES (OR 1 FULL-SIZE ONE)

⅓ cup / 60 g caperberries, plus 4 for garnish if making tea sandwiches

4 ounces / 115 g aged Cheddar

2 slices pullman (sandwich) bread

1 tablespoon Dijon mustard

Rinse the caperberries well, then soak them in warm water while you are readying the rest of the ingredients.

Cut the Cheddar into thin slices. Lightly toast the bread and cut off the crusts. Spread a thin layer of mustard on one side of each bread slice.

Chop about two-thirds of the caperberries and spread them on what will be the bottom bread slice. Follow with the Cheddar and top with the whole caperberries. Close the sandwich with the remaining bread slice, mustard side down.

If you are making tea sandwiches for your British mother-in-law, cut the sandwich along its two diagonals to yield four triangles and affix a toothpick with a caperberry garnish in each triangle. If this is your lunch, just dig in.

Eggplant, capers, and mint are a felicitous yet ubiquitous flavor combination whose parentage is impossible to attribute. I can't consciously call this recipe mine, but I can call it accessible and joyful. I like to use Japanese eggplants because they're virtually seedless and can be cut into just-the-right-size wheels. But feel free to use a different variety and slice it into manageable-size bites.

Ziti piccanti ai capperi, melanzane e menta
Spicy ziti with eggplant, capers, and mint

Fill a pot with 3 quarts / 3 L water, cover it, and set it over heat to come to a boil.

Put the capers into a tea strainer and run under hot water to melt away all the visible salt. Rinse well and leave to soak in warm water while you are readying the rest of the ingredients.

Slant the blade of your knife until it is almost parallel to the cutting board and use the heel of your hand to gently press the blade down on the garlic clove until you've cracked the skin. Peel the garlic clove and leave it whole.

Slice the eggplant as thinly as possible into rounds.

Pour 3 tablespoons of the olive oil into a frying pan large enough to hold the eggplant slices in a single layer and place it over medium heat. Place a plate next to the stove and line it with a paper towel. When the fragrance of the oil hits your nostrils decisively, add the eggplant and panfry for 3 to 4 minutes, until the slices become pliant and glossy. Lift a slice from the oil with tongs and if it has some brown caramelization spots, turn it over and panfry the other side. Transfer the eggplant slices to the paper-towel–lined plate.

Drain the capers and toss them into the oil used to cook the eggplant. Add the garlic clove, tomato concentrate, and 6 or 7 mint leaves and then douse with 2 cups / 475 ml hot water. Season with chili flakes to best suit your glee for heat—I like about ½ teaspoon—stir well to dilute the concentrate, turn the heat on to medium, and simmer until reduced by about one-third.

FOR 5 TO 6 PEOPLE

3 tablespoons capers packed in salt

1 garlic clove

1 Japanese eggplant (see headnote)

4 tablespoons / 60 ml extra-virgin olive oil

2 tablespoons tomato concentrate (or paste)

½ cup / 10 g loosely packed mint leaves

Red chili flakes

1 package (1 pound / 450 g) ziti

continued

The water should be boiling by now. Season it with 1 tablespoon salt, stir in the pasta, and cover the pot. Set a timer for 2 minutes shy of the suggested cooking time. When the water starts to boil again, remove the cover and adjust the heat so the water is at a lively, but not rolling, boil.

The sauce will be ready in the time it takes for the pasta to cook. It should be loosely velvety in appearance and runny but not watery. Sample the sauce and adjust the salt to your liking. Return the eggplant to the pan.

When the timer goes off, fish the ziti out of the water with a handheld strainer and add them to the sauce along with 2 to 3 tablespoons of the pasta cooking water. Raise the heat to the highest setting and swirl and jostle the pan for an additional minute or two to finish cooking the pasta.

Add the last tablespoon of olive oil and transfer to a warm platter. Garnish with the remaining mint and serve right away.

The emotional dimension of this dish is infinite in my life. In the long-ago summer lull of a boat, its fragrance wafting from below deck is the only thing that could keep my siblings and me still for more than five minutes. In my teen years, it finds a winter home in my newly divorced mother's kitchen. As I enter adulthood and move to New York, I tinker with it in a tiny kitchen where, with time, the swordfish changes some and eventually gains its name as a witness to the beginning of my love for my husband. I still remember the moment. Leonard Cohen was billowing about a man tied to a kitchen chair, and I recall panicking that my too-small-for-a-chair kitchen wouldn't be big enough to tie him down. I remember his hands between me and the stove, my clean hair caressing his nostrils. I remember that I never wanted that moment to end. It didn't. Twenty-two years later in San Francisco, this brightly hued combination of tomato, capers, and olives over swordfish is still the best-loved dish in my repertoire by both my husband and my son.

During my student days, when a swordfish steak per guest was more than I could afford, I stretched it with cubing and found that I could keep it moister if I cooked it partially and finished it in the hot sauce off the heat. It can, of course, be made with whole steaks, but they should be no more than ½ inch / 12 mm thick so they can cook all the way through without drying on the outside. You can use other fish, like halibut, hake, bass, tilapia, or even red mullet if you are lucky enough to find it. I always make some extra so I have leftovers to break up with a fork and use as spaghetti sauce the following day.

Pescespada dell'amore
Swordfish of love

Put the capers into a tea strainer and run under hot water to melt away all the visible salt. Rinse well and leave to soak in warm water while you are readying the rest of the ingredients.

Wash the brine off the olives well and pit them. Leave them to soak in warm water until ready to use.

Cut the swordfish into 1-inch / 2.5-cm cubes. Season the cubes all over with 1 teaspoon salt and a pinch of pepper.

continued

FOR 4 PEOPLE

2 tablespoons capers packed in salt

3 tablespoons Gaeta olives

1 pound / 450 g skinless swordfish steak

Salt and pepper

1 garlic clove

1 handful basil leaves

1 can (14 ounces / 400 g) peeled whole San Marzano tomatoes

4 tablespoons / 60 ml extra-virgin olive oil

1 teaspoon dried oregano

Red chili flakes (optional)

Slant the blade of your knife until it is almost parallel to the cutting board and use the heel of your hand to gently press the blade down on the garlic clove until you've cracked the skin. Peel the garlic clove and leave it whole.

Stack the basil leaves, roll them up tightly lengthwise, and slice them crosswise into thin ribbons. This technique will keep the basil from bruising and turning bitter.

Empty the can of tomatoes into a bowl. Fill the empty can with water and swirl it about to collect the tomato juice netting the sides of the can. Add it to the bowl. Crush the tomatoes with a potato masher or your hands until they are broken but still chunky.

Pour 2 tablespoons of the olive oil into a 10- to 12-inch sauté pan, add the garlic clove, and set over medium-low heat. When you see some tiny bubbling around the garlic clove, turn it to blister on the other side. When the oil is shimmery and its fragrance wafts up to your nose without you having to bend over the stove, remove and discard the garlic.

Raise the heat to medium-high and add the swordfish cubes. Sear quickly on all sides for 2 to 3 minutes, just until the fish changes from powder pink to milky gray. Lift the swordfish from the pan with a slotted spoon. Let the moisture fall back into the pan and put the fish on a plate.

Pour the remaining 2 tablespoons olive oil into the same pan over medium heat and scrape up the bits left by the swordfish on the pan bottom. Add half of the basil and the tomatoes, season with 1 teaspoon salt, and cook at a lively simmer for 10 to 12 minutes, until the tomatoes are no longer tangy.

Drain and squeeze the olives and capers, then stir them into the tomatoes. Cook for another 5 to 8 minutes, until the sauce is bright in color and taste and somewhat loose in appearance.

Turn off the heat and return the fish to the pan. Sprinkle with the oregano and stir. Taste the sauce and adjust salt and pepper to suit your palate. If you like a flash of heat, now is the time to add red chili flakes. Cover the pan with a tight-fitting lid and leave the swordfish in the hot sauce to finish cooking. In 15 to 20 minutes the fish will achieve tender perfection, and there it will stay as you take your time to ready the rest of the meal. This technique will keep the fish tender even if it stays on the stove for a while.

When ready to serve, pour everything onto a warm serving platter and garnish with the remaining basil.

Salads are never a recipe in my kitchen; they're the children of improvisation, ingenuity, experimentation, and, often, haste. This one is an exception. It was born in a May almost ten years ago. The combination of sweet, fresh, and tart dried cherries, fleshy caper leaves, snappy Little Gem leaves, and woodsy hazelnuts so enchanted palates that evening that I saved it in my repertoire and have served it at many dinners since.

Lattughino con ciliegie, foglie di cappero e nocciole tostate
Little Gems with cherries, caper leaves, and toasted hazelnuts

Soak the dried cherries in warm water to plump and soften while you are readying the rest of the ingredients.

Trim the bottom of each Little Gem head, then open the leaves and tear them into pieces that can be manageably eaten. I like to leave the smaller inner leaves whole. Drop the basil and Little Gem leaves into a salad spinner, cover with water, and leave to soak for a few minutes to allow the greens to release any grit. Repeat this step two or three times until the leaves aren't releasing any more dirt. Submerge the clean green leaves in water, toss 8 to 10 ice cubes into the spinner, and leave the greens to crisp while you ready the rest of the ingredients.

Thinly slice the shallot and place in a small bowl. Drizzle the slices with 3 tablespoons of the vinegar, add 2 ice cubes, and fill the bowl with cold water.

Halve and pit the fresh cherries. Rinse the caper leaves, stack them, roll them up tightly lengthwise, and slice them crosswise into thin ribbons. Roughly chop the hazelnuts.

Combine the fresh cherries, caper leaves, and hazelnuts in your salad bowl. Drain the dried cherries and, depending on their size, leave them whole or split them in half, then toss them into the salad bowl. Drain the lettuce and basil leaves and spin them dry three times, pouring out the water at the bottom of the bowl between one spin cycle and the next. Add to the salad bowl.

Season everything with 1 teaspoon salt and enough pepper to suit your taste. Toss well. Add the remaining 1 tablespoon vinegar and toss again. Pour in the olive oil from one side of the salad bowl, then toss again until the leaves are well coated. Sample a leaf, adjust the seasonings if necessary to suit your taste. Drain the shallot, scatter them over the salad,, and serve.

FOR 4 PEOPLE

2 tablespoons dried cherries

2 to 3 heads Little Gem lettuce (depending on the size)

1 cup / 25 g loosely packed taut basil leaves

½ small shallot

4 tablespoons / 60 ml red wine vinegar

1 cup / 130 g fresh cherries

8 to 10 caper leaves

2 tablespoons toasted hazelnuts

Salt and pepper

3 tablespoons extra-virgin olive oil

Back in the 1980s, rabbit was not a selection obvious to the butcher in the Upper East Side neighborhood to which I had moved straight from the Umbrian countryside, so I used chicken instead. The day the local Lebanese fruiterer was out of green olives, I bought some sun-dried black ones in their place. I added orange zest later, as my hand in the kitchen became surer of itself. And that is how the rabbit with green olives of my youth was reincarnated into the family favorite chicken. Instead of buying a whole chicken, you can use parts. Dark meat is always juicier, but if you prefer breast, braise it 6 to 8 minutes less or it will be dry. Rosemary, savory, or thyme is a good stand-in for sage, and any type of black olive will do. And it goes without saying that you can and should use rabbit if you like it and can source it.

Pollo con olive nere al profumo di salvia e arancio
Sage and orange–scented chicken with black olives

FOR 6 TO 8 PEOPLE

1 chicken, 4 to 5 pounds / 1.8 to 2.2 kg

Salt and pepper

1 cup / 170 g black olives

1 orange

4 sage sprigs

3 garlic cloves

Extra-virgin olive oil as needed

1 cup / 240 ml white wine

1 cup / 240 ml chicken stock, heated

The day before making the dish, ask your butcher to cut the chicken into 10 pieces (2 legs, 2 thighs, 2 wings, and 2 bone-in breast halves, each split in half). Make sure the back ends up in the package, too, as it will impart great flavor to the final dish. When you get home, sprinkle the chicken pieces on all sides with salt, cover, and refrigerate.

About an hour before you start cooking, take the seasoned chicken pieces out of the refrigerator, pat them dry, and leave them on the counter to come to room temperature.

Wash the brine off the olives well and place them in a small bowl. Squeeze each one lightly with your fingers to loosen the flesh from the pit and discard the pits. Cut 2 wide strips of peel from the orange. Rub 2 of the sage sprigs and the orange peel strips between your palms to release their essence and add them to the bowl.

Slant the blade of your knife until it is almost parallel to the cutting board and use the heel of your hand to gently press the blade down on 2 of the garlic cloves until you've cracked the skin. Peel the cloves and leave them whole. Keep one aside and add the other one to the olives. Pour enough oil into the bowl to barely cover the olives and toss well.

continued

Grate 1½ teaspoons zest from the orange. Peel the remaining garlic clove, then mince it into a paste with a generous pinch of salt. Mix the garlic and grated zest together. Rub the remaining 2 sage sprigs between your palms to release their essence.

Select a sauté pan wide enough to accommodate the chicken pieces in one cozy, but comfortable, layer. Pour 2 to 3 tablespoons olive oil into the pan, add the whole peeled garlic clove, and over low heat slowly coax out the garlic's fragrance.

Remove and discard the garlic, raise the heat to medium, and add the chicken pieces. Brown them for 5 to 7 minutes, until the chicken will lift off the pan without being forced or pulled. It should be golden. Turn the chicken pieces over and repeat the step on the other side, then move them to a plate.

Turn the heat back down to low, toss in the garlic-zest mixture and sage sprigs, and stir to coat them in chicken deliciousness until the garlic has softened. It will take a couple of minutes, and be careful not to burn the garlic. Return the chicken to the pan, raise the heat to high, and douse with the wine. When the acid of the alcohol no longer pinches your throat and punches your nose and its sugar sweetly caresses your eyes and cheeks instead, pour the hot stock over the chicken. The liquid should lap just the bottom one-quarter of the chicken.

Lower the heat until the stock is simmering with a low, gentle mutter. Cover partially and cook for 30 to 35 minutes. During cooking, you will visit with your chicken every 7 minutes or so to stir it and ensure it has between one half- and 1-inch liquid and isn't sticking to the bottom of the pan. If necessary, add a little hot water. It is important that there be enough liquid to have a good amount of sauce, but not so much that the chicken is boiling instead of braising.

When the chicken is about 10 minutes from ready, fish the garlic clove, orange peel strips, and sage out of the olives and drain off most of the marinating oil. Stir the olives into the pan and finish cooking the chicken.

The chicken is ready when it starts to barely retract from the joints and bones without falling away and is quite tender. It should look lustrous, luscious, and moist and smell like this is the last dish you'll want to eat before dying.

Sample the sauce and adjust salt and pepper to your taste. Use tongs to attractively arrange the chicken pieces on a warm serving platter, douse with the sauce and olives, and serve.

In meat braises, cracked bones give unique and unadulterated depth and flavor unmatched by even the best stock. This simple, basic tip is one that a decade plus of my students list among the ones to have most significantly impacted their cooking. I am lucky enough to have a butcher that will divide lamb shoulder into pieces cracking through the bone, but often lamb shoulder is cut and packed in stew-size bites. If that is all you can find, ask your butcher for a cracked lamb bone, toss it into the pan with the lamb, and adjust the cooking time to the size of the meat pieces.

Spalla d'agnello alle olive verdi
Lamb shoulder with green olives

Ask your butcher to cut the lamb into 8 pieces, cracking through the bones and trimming excess fat. The day before making the dish, sprinkle about 2 teaspoons salt on all sides of the lamb pieces, then cover and refrigerate. The next day, take the meat out of the refrigerator, uncover it, and let it come to room temperature while you ready the rest of the ingredients.

Cut the onions in half from stem to root end. Place an onion half cut side down on a cutting board with the stem to root line perpendicular to you. With a sharp knife, go all across the onion dome from right to left—or left to right if you are left-handed—cutting the onion into thin scythes. Repeat with the remaining onion halves. Strip the leaves off the marjoram sprigs and mince them.

Pour 3 tablespoons of the olive oil into a shallow saucepan in which the lamb pieces will fit in one cozy but comfortable layer and set over medium heat. Hover your hand over the pan; when it feels uncomfortable, it is time to add the lamb. Brown one side of the meat to a light golden brown. When you can lift it off the pan without forcefully pulling it, turn it over and brown the other side. Move the lamb pieces to a plate.

Add the remaining 1 tablespoon olive oil, the sliced onions, and half of the marjoram to the pan. Turn down the heat to low, sprinkle with 1 teaspoon salt, add 2 to 3 tablespoons warm water, and scrape up the brown bits from the pan bottom. Cook the onions for about 15 minutes, until soft, fragrant, and hazy. Stir occasionally to ensure they don't stick to the bottom of the pan.

continued

FOR 4 PEOPLE

1 bone-in lamb shoulder, 3 pounds / 1.4 kg

Salt and pepper

3 red onions

2 marjoram sprigs

4 tablespoons / 60 ml extra-virgin olive oil

1 cup / 240 ml dry white wine

½ cup / 90 g green olives (Castelvetrano or Cerignola)

3 anchovy fillets packed in oil

½ teaspoon red chili flakes

Spalla d'agnello alle olive verdi, continued

Return the lamb to the pan and raise the heat to high. Douse with the wine and let it evaporate until it stops punching your nose and starts caressing your eyes. Add enough warm water to lap the bottom one-third of the lamb. Once the liquid boils, turn down the heat to low, cover the pan with a tight-fitting lid, and braise the lamb for about 40 minutes, until the meat starts retracting from the bone. Check periodically to make sure there is always about 1 inch / 2.5 cm of water at the bottom. This should be a saucy dish.

Wash the brine off the olives well, then pit them and chop them roughly. Add them to the lamb and continue the braising for an additional 20 minutes. If the sauce is very watery, leave the lid off; otherwise, position it so it is halfway off.

In the meantime, mince together the anchovies and red chili flakes.

When the lamb is ready—the meat should be very tender but not falling off the bone—move the lamb to a warm shallow serving bowl, top with the minced anchovies and chili, and garnish with the remaining marjoram. Serve warm to hot.

CEREALI /
CEREALS

CHAPTER 4

RISO / RICE

A vibrant, unexpected life beyond risotto

Rice was a bane in childhood. *Riso in bianco*—"rice dressed in white," or, more accurately, naked, save a teaspoon of olive oil—meant I was sick and stuck in bed. Windows open to air out germs brought further torment as my siblings' joyful racket breezed in from the garden. One afternoon—I must have been ten or eleven—at the tail end of a pesky respiratory ailment, I came into the kitchen to find my brother in deep querying conversation with my mother, their heads bowed over a bubbling pot. Filippo was pauselessly stirring with a wooden spoon practicing risotto skills as he intended to woo a crush with a dinner of Champagne risotto. Cooked right, it turned out, rice was a love potion.

Rice, native to the Far East, comes to Italy via the Arab world. It migrates to Sicily as early as the ninth century and later gains a foothold in northern Italy thanks to the trade ways of Venice. Until the early twentieth century, Italians ate *riso nostrale*—homegrown or national rice—a short, round rice. In 1925, enterprising farmers and curious agronomists cross *riso nostrale* with Lady Wright, a long-grain American variety, creating a tapered and wide grain with less soluble starch. Risotto, as we know it today, is born.

But before we Italians ate wavy, glistening risotto, we found comfort in rice soups. We steamed it hot in the winter and rinsed it cold in the summer. We baked it into timbales, crowns, cakes, and tarts. We deep-fried it into *arancine* and *supplì*. And we still do. According to rice sommelier Valentina Masotti, only 25 percent of the 600,000 acres (245,000 hectares) of Italy dedicated to this cereal are for risotto varieties. The rest is made up of 150-plus cultivars suited for everything from sushi to pilaf to flour. This remarkable diversity makes Italy the number-one producer of rice in the European Union.

Over 90 percent of Italian rice is grown in the plains of Piedmont and Lombardy, which are home to the only Italian PDO rice, riso di Baraggia, an area riding parts of the Piedmontese provinces of Biella and Vercelli where seven varieties of rice are grown. Veneto is the next region for rice cultures, with two PGI productions. The Po River delta is home to several cultivars prized for the minerality derived from the convergence of fresh- and saltwater. Verona has a protected unique rice breed called Vialone Nano. A small number of niche producers can be found in southern Tuscany, Calabria, Sicily, and Sardinia.

Italian rice varieties in US markets are mostly Arborio and Carnaroli. Developed in the middle of the twentieth century, they are considered the best for risotto. Carnaroli, the prince of rice, is valued for its ability to absorb flavorful liquid while keeping bite and releasing the right amount of starch to create the elusive creamy wave. Retaining texture in cooking makes Arborio and Carnaroli adaptable to techniques other than risotto.

A few other kinds of Italian rice are available in specialty shops. Vialone Nano and Baldo, are risotto varieties. Venere and Artemide, are versatile black cultivars with strong nutty, floral fragrances that go well with vegetables, stinky cheeses, and seafood.

Rice will last for twelve to eighteen months on a shelf if vacuum sealed. Once opened, it should be used within three months. Always sniff rice before using it. It should smell lightly of chalk and barely accumulated dust. If you perceive rancidity or a note of dead mosquitoes and cobwebs, toss it.

When buying rice imported from Italy, look at the packaging. Do you see information about the crop's provenance? Are there any modifiers following the variety of rice, say, Carnaroli Riserva rather than just Carnaroli? Does the box bear the EU blue-and-gold or red-and-gold seal of quality? Does it bear the branding of a local consortium? These are all indicators of rice that is produced not only according to the transparency required by Italian law but also with mindfulness and care for the crop, its territory, and those who make it and eat it.

Among the Italian dishes of which rice is the protagonist, risotto is not just the best known but also the most alluring. It conjures style, elegance, the murmured laughter of well-heeled fashion types around the table of a sleek Milanese restaurant. This ineffable allure makes risotto seem challenging. Even the most accomplished home cook can become nervous about risotto. In reality, this iconic dish is as elementary in execution as it is impressive. In fact, my risotto technique—hatched in professional kitchens and honed for the cooking classroom—dumbs it down to the level of a thirty-minute weeknight meal.

I warn you that you are about to embark on a learning journey that challenges the diktats of the majority and likely years of your own tightly held beliefs. But I guarantee that by eschewing the tenets of complex stocks and constant stirring, you will compose a deeply and cleanly flavored risotto with minimum effort.

Hold my hand and let's go.

Let's start with the recipe for a basic risotto whose driving flavors are parmigiano and butter. Then, while you are eating it, read on for tips on building a one-ingredient stock that extracts the unencumbered quintessence of whatever inspires your risotto art that day.

Del risotto
On risotto

FOR 4 PEOPLE

Salt and pepper

1 small shallot

4 tablespoons / 60 g unsalted butter

1 cup / 200 g rice for risotto

1 cup / 240 ml dry white wine, at room temperature

½ cup / 120 ml grated parmigiano reggiano

Fill a saucepan with 5 cups / 1.2 L water, season it with 2 teaspoons salt, and bring to just below the boiling point. Cover and keep hot over the lowest heat setting. While the water is coming to a boil, ready the rest of the equipment and ingredients.

Roughly chop the shallot, sprinkle it with ½ teaspoon salt, then mince it into a paste.

Arm yourself with a wooden spoon, a wide saucepan or sauté pan no deeper than 4 inches / 10 cm, and a ladle. Warm four dinner plates for serving the risotto.

Line up the ingredients next to the stove in order of appearance: 2 tablespoons of the butter, the shallot, rice, wine, and pepper. Have salt handy, should you need it. Keep the remaining butter and 2 tablespoons of the cheese a little farther away, ready for finishing. Pour the rest of the parmigiano into a small bowl to serve later.

Plop the 2 tablespoons butter into the saucepan and melt it over medium heat until it starts foaming in the center and has pale-yellow, small bubbles at the edges. Add the shallot-salt paste and sauté, stirring often, until it is quite soft, hazy, and shiny—almost coming undone. It should take 3 to 5 minutes, depending on how finely you minced the shallot.

Stir the rice into the butter and shallot and set a timer for 20 minutes. Twenty minutes is considered the perfect timing from when the rice first touches heat. Stir the rice continuously to coat it in deliciousness for 1 to 2 minutes. The rice will become shiny and translucent and will lose its lightly dusty smell. Raise the heat to high and pour in the wine. When the wine no longer smells acidic and caresses rather than curls your nose, add 4 cups / 950 ml of the hot salted water. It will come to a boil almost immediately.

Lower the heat until the rice is at a lively bubble but not boiling so hard that its surface is covered with steam and you cannot see the grains. You will need to stay close to the stove, but there will be no need to stir; just move it occasionally to check that it isn't sticking. You can use this time to toss together a salad or set the table.

At minute 10, the rice grains will have grown considerably, and the water will be cloudy but still quite soupy.

At about minute 15, taste for salt and adjust as necessary. The liquid will be detectably starchy, and the rice will be close to the surface but barely visible. If the tips of the rice grains peek above the surface of the liquid, add a ladleful of the hot salted water.

At minute 18, the rice should be peeking above the surface and the liquid tightening but still very runny. If it is too dense, add a little hot salted water. Stay close, wooden spoon in hand.

By minute 20, the rice should be fully visible; the grains will be together but separate and can easily be moved around the pan.

There can be elements at play that affect the 20-minute standard by 1 or 2 minutes either way: a drafty kitchen, older rice. But most of all, your taste. At 20 minutes, the rice will be cooked through but quite al dente. If you prefer a softer bite, give it a little extra time; if you prefer some soul, stop at 19 minutes.

continued

Turn off the heat and vigorously stir in the remaining 2 tablespoons butter and the 2 tablespoons cheese.

Your risotto should be creamy and wavy—all'onda is the jargon—easily falling from a serving spoon in a continuous ribbon. Put it on a plate and tilt the plate. It should slide down quickly and uniformly. If it plops, if you have to shake the spoon for it to fall, or if it doesn't move easily down the plate, the risotto is too dense. You can loosen it with a little of the hot salted water.

Divide the risotto among the four warm dinner plates and swirl the plates around to form a flat circle. Lightly dust with pepper and serve immediately with the remaining cheese on the side.

Now sit down to eat and let's chat about stock. As my palate became more exacting, I started noticing all risotto tasted the same and was only as good as the stock used to make it. A handful of peas or mushrooms was an afterthought, not the defining profile I expected from the description.

I started playing with very diluted stocks enriched with the scraps of whatever I was using. For example, artichoke leaves for an artichoke risotto, or roasted pumpkin skin for a pumpkin risotto. I soon noticed I wasn't the only one doing this; other women in the kitchen were veering the same way. Eventually, I was emboldened enough to use only hot water to extract the flavor of the day.

The best flavor combination to test your revamped risotto method is lemon and rosemary. Drop a sprig of rosemary and a couple of lemon peel strips into the hot salted water. Mince a few rosemary needles and combine them with grated lemon zest and pepper to taste. Use the flavored water to cook the risotto. Garnish with the rosemary–lemon zest mince and sprinkle with a few drops of lemon juice. Eat the risotto before you send me a thank-you note.

Other ideas for flavoring your stock are shrimp carapaces with empty pea pods, smashed asparagus stems with marjoram, dried porcini with saffron, tomato with cracked lamb bones, and radicchio leaves with celery seeds. In other words, the sky and your imagination are your only limits. Go play.

My mother was somewhere over the Great Lakes when I had the kind of contractions that foretold Ernesto was a-coming. It took another two days of labor for him to actually show up; he marched to his own tempo from the start. But he must have felt it was safe to enter the scene now that his *nonna* had arrived to mind the beginning of his life. From that bleary-eyed time, I remember little, but the cabbage and rice soup that my mother deemed essential for lactating and breastfeeding has woven itself forever into my cooking repertoire. Use whatever cabbage you prefer and is in season. Cauliflower leaves also work well. Through the years, I added various flavors and landed on toasted cumin seeds as my favorite.

Minestra di riso e cavolo
Rice and cabbage soup

Shred the cabbage and set aside a handful for the garnish. Slice the shallot paper-thin. Heat a small frying pan over medium heat until hovering a hand over it feels uncomfortable. Toss in the cumin seeds, lift the pan off the heat, and swirl it around to lightly toast them so their fragrance can bloom. Chop them roughly.

Pour the olive oil into a saucepan, then add the cabbage, shallot, and cumin. Season with 1 teaspoon salt and turn on the heat to medium-low. Cover so that the vegetables can wilt and release liquid in which they will braise for 15 to 20 minutes, until fragrant and tender. Stir occasionally to make sure they do not stick and add a little warm water if necessary.

Add the rice and pour in enough warm water to submerge all the ingredients by ½ inch / 12 mm. Simmer for about 15 minutes, until the rice is quite tender and the soup is dense but runny. Taste and adjust salt to your taste. My mother added no pepper as she was sure Ernesto wouldn't like it, but you can, of course.

Ladle into warm bowls, garnish with the raw cabbage shreds, and finish with a thread of olive oil. Serve warm.

FOR 4 PEOPLE

¼ head cabbage

1 shallot

½ teaspoon cumin seeds

2 tablespoons extra-virgin olive oil, plus more for finishing

Salt

1 heaping cup / 220 g short- or medium-grain rice

Rice timbales were common dinner-party fare in my family home. They are easy to make, can be prepared in advance and heated at the last moment, and they never fail to draw wows from the dining audience. This version calls for pumpkin, an ingredient that I have learned to appreciate as a cook in America, as it is not traditional in my home region of Umbria. Pumpkin is quite common in the cooking of the Veneto region, however, from where the cheese in the recipe also hails. If you cannot find Monte Veronese cheese, any good melty cheese, like a gruyère, a fontina, or even a young Cheddar, will do.

Corona di riso alla zucca e Monte Veronese
Rice crown with pumpkin and Monte Veronese cheese

FOR A 9- TO 10-INCH / 23- TO 25-CM RING MOLD; FOR 8 TO 10 PEOPLE

1 small pumpkin or winter squash, about 1½ pounds / 680 g

Salt and pepper

1 cup / 200 g Arborio rice

1 egg

1 cup / 240 ml cream

1 tablespoon unsalted butter

¼ cup / 30 g unseasoned dried breadcrumbs

1 cup / 120 g packed shredded Monte Veronese cheese

⅓ cup grated parmigiano reggiano

Nutmeg, for grating

Heat the oven to 350°F / 180°C / gas mark 4. Halve the pumpkin. Roast it cut side down for 25 to 30 minutes, until it opposes no resistance to the piercing of a knife.

Bring 1 quart / 1 L water to a boil in a saucepan and season it with 1½ teaspoons salt. Stir in the rice and cook at a low boil for about 15 minutes, until tender and soulful. Drain the rice and spread it on a plate to cool.

When the pumpkin is cool enough to handle, discard the seeds and filaments. Scoop out the flesh into a bowl, mash it with a fork, and cool completely.

Whisk the egg and cream together. Grease a 9- to 10-inch / 23- to 25-cm ring mold with the butter and dust with the breadcrumbs. Swirl the mold to coat it evenly then turn it over to shake off the excess.

Measure 1½ cups / 370 g of the pumpkin puree into a bowl. Add the cold rice and season with salt and pepper to suit your palate. Stir in the cheeses and the egg-cream mixture. Stand by the bowl and grate nutmeg into it just until its fragrance wafts up to your nostrils. Stir to distribute the seasoning evenly.

Pour the mixture into the mold and tap it on the counter to settle. Loosely tent with aluminum foil and bake for about 40 minutes, until it feels a little bouncy but not jiggly and the rice is beginning to shirk away from the sides.

Let the mold cool for 5 minutes, then slide a knife around the outside and inside edges of the ring. Invert onto a flat plate and gently shake to loosen the crown. Hold your breath, cross your fingers, and lift the mold. The crown almost always comes out whole, but should it be uncooperative, do not fret. Just scoop out the stuck pieces and patch up the ring; it will still be delicious. Serve warm.

This dish is ubiquitous in Italian summers. Everyone has their own version, with ingredients ranging from fresh vegetables to cocktail onions, from ham to sliced hot dogs, from soft young pecorino to cheese singles. The dressing has some mayonnaise. It is such a common preparation that premade mixes for rice salad are a thing on supermarket shelves. My version of rice salad is a direct descendant of my mother's. The only pickles are a few cornichons, olives are just a garnish, all the vegetables are fresh, and mayonnaise is just a decoration while the main dressing is olive oil. I select rice that holds cooking well, and I rinse it both before and after cooking to keep the rice grains from clumping. My proteins of choice are crumbled canned tuna and/or wedges of hard-boiled egg, but you can also opt for diced ham and Swiss cheese. Just promise to stay away from the hot dogs.

Insalata di riso
Rice salad

Heat the oven to 350°F / 180°C / gas mark 4. Place the bell pepper on a sheet pan, then slide it into the hot oven. Roast for about 25 minutes, until the skin has burnt spots and the pepper has begun to collapse and wrinkle. Grab the pepper with tongs, drop it into a brown paper bag, roll the top of the bag closed, and let sit for 10 minutes. Enclosing it in the bag will make the pepper easy to peel.

While the pepper is roasting, bring 1 quart / 1 L water to a boil in a saucepan and season it with 1 tablespoon salt. Rinse the rice in a bowl of cold water, drain it, then drop it into the boiling water. Turn down the heat until the water is gently but visibly bubbling. Cover partially and set a timer for 15 minutes. When the timer goes off, taste the rice. It should be firm but not crunchy. If necessary, cook it for a minute or two longer. When the rice is ready, drain it into the colander and cool it with running water. Tip it into a serving bowl.

FOR 6 PEOPLE

1 yellow or red bell pepper

Salt and pepper

1½ cups / 300 g medium- or long-grain rice

2 medium zucchini

4 ounces / 115 g tender string beans

2 medium carrots

3 eggs

1 tablespoon vinegar (any kind)

8 cornichons, or 1½ tablespoons capers in vinegar

1 cup / 150 g cherry tomatoes

6 chives

continued

½ cup / 10 g loosely
packed basil leaves
(parsley or mint also works)

1 can (5 to 6 ounces /
140 to 170 g) tuna
in olive oil

½ lemon

Extra-virgin olive oil
as needed

¼ cup / 60 ml mayonnaise

1½ tablespoons
black olives

½ avocado

Bring 2 quarts / 2 L water to a boil in a saucepan and season it with 1½ teaspoons salt. Fill a medium bowl half full with water and add 1 handful of ice cubes to it.

Drop the zucchini into the boiling water and cook for 5 to 10 minutes, depending on size, until just tender and still bright in color. Fish the zucchini out of the water with a handheld strainer and immerse them in the ice water.

Add the string beans to the boiling water and cook for 6 to 8 minutes, depending on size, until tender and still bright green. Transfer them to the ice water.

It's the carrots' turn next, so peel them while the beans are cooking. When the beans are out of the water, plop in the carrots and cook for 5 to 6 minutes, depending on size, until just tender. Add them to the ice water.

As each batch of vegetables cools down, lift it out of the water and, if necessary, add more ice cubes to the bowl to keep the water cold.

Lastly, gently slide the eggs into the boiling water and add the vinegar. Should an egg crack, the vinegar will cause the white to coagulate and keep it from seeping out. Once the water comes back to a boil, give the eggs 3 minutes, then turn off the heat. Cover the pan and set the timer for 11 minutes. When the timer goes off, cool the eggs in the ice water.

When the vegetables are cold, slice the zucchini into rounds or half-moons (depending on their diameter) ⅛ inch / 3 mm thick. Cut each string bean on a slight slant into 3 to 4 little logs, eliminating the stem. Dice the carrots into ¼-inch / 6-mm cubes.

Peel the roasted pepper, cut it in half, and remove the core, filaments, and seeds. Slice it into strips ½ inch / 12 mm wide along the ribbing, then divide each strip into 2 or 3 pieces. Cut the tomatoes in half or into quarters if they are on the larger side. Rinse and slice the cornichons (or rinse the capers).

Slice the chives into thin rings. Set aside 3 or 4 basil leaves for garnishing. Stack the rest, roll them up tightly lengthwise, and slice them crosswise into thin ribbons. (If you are using mint, it can be prepped the same way; if using parsley, keep a few leaves for garnish and finely chop the rest.)

Set aside a few tomato halves and 7 to 9 string bean pieces for garnishing, then add all the rest of the prepped vegetables and sliced herbs to the rice.

Peel the eggs, cut 2 eggs into 8 wedges each, and add them to the rice bowl. Thinly slice the remaining egg into rounds and set it aside for garnish.

Drain off the oil from the tuna and flake it with a fork. Add the tuna to the rice bowl and toss all the ingredients well to distribute them evenly.

Sample the mix, season with salt and pepper to best suit your palate, and toss. Sprinkle with the juice of the lemon half and toss again to spread the seasoning throughout. Douse with a generous 2 to 3 tablespoons olive oil and toss well again. Sample the rice one last time to be sure the seasoning pleases you.

Transfer the rice salad to a serving bowl and even the surface with a dinner knife or spatula so it is slightly mounded in the center. Spread the mayonnaise in a thin layer over the rice.

Rinse and pit the olives and pit, peel, and slice the avocado. Create a fanciful pattern on the mayonnaise layer using the olives, avocado slices, and all the ingredients—egg slices, tomato halves, string beans, and basil leaves—you set aside. Cover and refrigerate until ready to serve.

I attribute this dish to my friend Micaela Malingri, who first made it for me to combat the torrid heat of a summer afternoon in Palo Alto, just south of San Francisco. In turn, she attributes it to a homestyle restaurant in Milan she used to frequent with her parents. Whatever its origin, I have fallen in love with the communal nature of this recipe, with its vivid colors and lively flavors, and cannot get enough of it. Use very ripe tomatoes, the ones that appeal to fruit flies. I prefer large, sweet heirloom varieties, like Cherokee Purple or Beefsteak. I use chives to give an allium touch, but if you like a more decisive hint, experiment with some shallot or even a clove or two of garlic. Basil is always a good bet with tomatoes, but you can mix in some mint and/or parsley and liven it up with a little marjoram or oregano.

Riso freddo estivo al pomodoro e basilico
Cold summer rice with tomatoes and basil

FOR 4 TO 5 PEOPLE

2 pounds / 1 kg overripe sweet tomatoes

Salt

1½ cups / 300 g Arborio rice

8 to 10 chives

1 cup / 20 g loosely packed basil leaves (see headnote for other herbs)

Black pepper or red chili flakes

Extra-virgin olive oil as needed

Bring 2 quarts / 2 L water to a boil in a saucepan. Fill a large bowl half full with water and drop 2 handfuls of ice cubes into it.

Score a skin deep X on the butt of each tomato with the tip of a paring knife. Drop the tomatoes into the boiling water for 1 to 2 minutes, until their skins are imperceptibly lifting and retracting at the Xs. Fish out the tomatoes with tongs or a slotted spoon and plop them into the ice bath.

Season the water in the pan with 1½ teaspoons salt. When it comes back to a boil, stir in the rice and then adjust the heat to keep the rice at a lively simmer. Set a timer for 15 minutes.

When the tomatoes have cooled down completely, you will be able to easily peel off the skins. Core the peeled tomatoes, cut them into chunks, and toss them into a food processor. Add most of the chives and basil leaves, saving a few for garnishing, and season with 1 teaspoon salt. Pulse until you have a dense and textured puree.

Transfer the puree to a serving bowl. Taste and adjust with salt and black pepper—or red chili flakes for a spicy kick—to suit your palate. Stir in 2 to 3 tablespoons olive oil, then taste and add more oil or seasonings if needed.

When the timer goes off, taste the rice. It should be al dente but not crunchy. When it is ready, drain it into a tight-mesh colander and run it under cold water to cool it and wash off some of the starch. Mound it in a shallow bowl and garnish it with the herbs you saved. Place the two bowls side by side in the middle of the table and invite diners to serve themselves.

When given the challenge to revive the small family farm in 2011 in the wet plains outside the Piedmontese city of Novara, my friend Cristina Cavalchini set on rice knowing she'd have to compete on quality. The commitment and investment paid off, and today Cristina owns and runs Riso Buono. Her extraordinary Carnaroli Riserva is the rice of choice for starred chefs all over the world. But I am a die-hard devotee of Artemide, an heirloom, long-grain black rice variety that she has single-handedly put back on the map, and is now widely available online. Unlike the plain canvas that are its white counterparts, Artemide has an enveloping scent and a flavor so complete it only needs scant, delicate elements to complement it.

Riso nero Artemide con gamberi e crema di avocado e dragoncello
Artemide black rice with shrimp and avocado tarragon cream

Rinse the rice and place it in a pot with 1 quart / 1 L water and 1 teaspoon salt. Bring to a boil, then lower the heat to a simmer and cover partially. Set a timer for 35 minutes. Check the rice periodically to make sure it has enough liquid, adding a little warm water if the rice sounds a little crackly and is beginning to stick to the pan.

Fill a small saucepan with water. Add 2 slices of lemon, 1 sprig of tarragon, and 1 teaspoon salt, then bring to a boil. Drop in the shrimp, cover the pan, and turn off the heat.

For the avocado cream, rinse the capers well in hot water. Pick the tarragon leaves from the remaining sprigs, saving a few pretty leaves for garnishing. Halve and pit the avocado, then spoon the flesh into a food processor.

Add the capers, tarragon leaves, and 1 tablespoon olive oil to the avocado, squeeze in a few drops of juice from the lemon, and process into a smooth puree. Sample the avocado cream and season with pepper to suit your taste.

When the timer goes off, taste the rice. It should be tender, with a bite that is firm but not crunchy. Cook for a little longer if necessary. Drain the rice and dress it with a few drops of olive oil while still warm.

Divide the rice evenly among four dinner plates. Drain the shrimp, arrange one or two on each plate, and then top with a spoonful of avocado cream. Garnish with the saved tarragon leaves and top with the sliced almonds. Serve warm with a bowl of the remaining avocado cream.

FOR 4 PEOPLE

1½ cups / 300 g Artemide rice

Salt and pepper

1 small lemon

4 or 5 tarragon sprigs

4 large or 8 medium shelled shrimp

1 tablespoon capers packed in salt

1 very ripe avocado

Extra-virgin olive oil as needed

2 tablespoons sliced almonds

Rice desserts are found throughout Italy. I favor the custardy ones of northern Tuscany—think rice pudding but with eggs. There are many versions—some in a crust, some layered straight onto the pan, some with added flavors—and all are delicious. I have culled mine from the many I have tried, enlisting the technical help of Sandra Rossi, owner of La Focaccia di Focette, the best focacceria in the coastal area of Versilia. Any kind of rice works for this sweet, but short-grain kernels give in to "custard-iness," while long-grain ones stay more textured. If fresh cherries are out of season, you can use cherries canned in water.

Budino di riso con ciliegie e amaretti al profumo di arancio
Orange-scented rice pudding with cherry and amaretti

FOR 4 PEOPLE

4 cups / 950 ml whole milk

1 lemon

½ teaspoon salt

½ cup / 100 g rice (see headnote)

1 cup / 130 g cherries

8 amaretti

3 tablespoons diced candied orange peel

4 eggs

⅓ cup / 70 g natural cane sugar

2½ teaspoons ground cinnamon

2 teaspoons almond extract

1 tablespoon rum (or other liquor)

Unsalted butter, to grease the baking dish

Pour the milk into a saucepan. Use a peeler to remove 3 wide strips of peel from the lemon and drop them into the milk. Heat the milk over medium heat to just below boiling, let it cool completely, and remove the lemon peel.

In the meantime, fill a saucepan with 1 quart / 1 L water and bring it to a boil. Season it with ½ teaspoon salt and stir in the rice. Turn the heat down to a simmer and set a timer for 10 minutes. When the timer goes off, drain the rice and spread it on a sheet pan to cool completely.

Heat the oven to 350°F / 180°C / gas mark 4.

Pit the cherries, crumble the amaretti, and rinse the candied orange peel to remove sugar and preservatives. Beat the eggs and sugar together in a bowl until lighter in color, smooth, and foamy. Stir in the cinnamon, almond extract, and rum, then whisk in the cooled milk.

Butter a 9-inch / 23-cm square or round baking dish. Spread the rice on the bottom of the dish and pat it down to level it. Scatter the cherries and orange peel over the rice and dust with the crumbled amaretti.

Pour the egg-milk mixture over the rice and slide the baking dish into the oven. Bake for 45 minutes to 1 hour, until the pudding is set and a toothpick inserted into the center comes out damp but clean. Serve warm to room temperature.

To make individual puddings, you can use mini Bundt pans or ramekins. Reduce the baking time by about half and look for the same signs of doneness.

CHAPTER 5

POLENTA

Centuries of sustenance for the peasants of Northeastern Italy
catapulted to the world stage

Adaptable, comforting, fragrant, generous—polenta's sensorial traits sound uncannily like the qualities one might seek in a life partner. The uses for this flavorful corn-based porridge span from budget-conscious, simple meals for a large family to elegant offerings at an intimate dinner party. In savory and sweet preparations and with different textures, polenta holds countless memories for generations of Italians.

Etymologically derived from the Latin *puls*—also the root for the word pulses—polenta has been around since ancient times as a mix of ground cereals and/or legumes with occasional appearances by wild seasonal foods. What we know as polenta today—corn dried, ground into a coarse meal, and cooked in water until tender—is the latest incarnation of this staple. Indeed, corn's tenure in the European diet started when European settlers invaded the continents known today as the Americas and were exposed to it.

On the Italian peninsula, this resilient crop found a particularly welcoming home in the cold valleys of the north. While still more popular in the upper half of the country, today polenta has become a well-loved ingredient of national fame.

Polenta owes its unique, engaging texture to the hardy breed of corn used to make it and the way it is milled. Flint corn has a rounded-top kernel that keeps its shape as it dries, thanks to the outer skin fully wrapping the endosperm. (For reference, American grits use dent corn, named after the dent that forms as the partially covered kernels dry.) To become polenta, flint corn undergoes reduction milling, repeated grinding that yields gradually smaller and more uniform granules for even cooking. Because the technique produces very low heat, the flavor and texture of the corn remain intact.

The most prized variety of flint corn for milling polenta is Ottofile, which translates as "eight rows." The ears have eight rows of kernels of a deep yellow, almost orange color. Ottofile is a rather low-yield crop, and today most polenta is ground from flint corn with higher yields. If you do come across a polenta that is made with Ottofile corn, it is definitely worth the premium price. One of my favorite producers is Anson Mills in South Carolina.

Two heirloom productions of particular note are Oro Rosso di Storo (Storo's Red Gold), a hyperlocal production in Trentino with small ears that are red orange, and Farina di Mais Marano (Marano's Maize Flour), a specialized crop in the Veneto province of Vicenza. Both these micro productions have been put back on the map by the determination of small farmers to stay relevant and a renewed interest in heirloom products. So far, they are not available on US market shelves, but they are well worth the suitcase space the next time you're in Italy.

Polenta is ground in a range of ways: *integrale*, or whole-grain; *bramata*, or coarsely ground; and fioretto, or finely ground. And because cooking times are long, it is common to buy polenta that has been either partly or completely cooked in advance and then dried again. *Precotta* has been partially precooked, while istantanea has been fully precooked. These last two options gain in convenience what they lose in texture.

You surely have been seeing yellow so far, as *polenta gialla*—"yellow polenta"—is the most ubiquitous kind. If your pantry only has space for one polenta, this is your fair-weather choice. It is readily available in any market and can be used for any dish that calls for polenta. But there are more kids in the polenta family.

In second place for popularity, though first in my heart, is *polenta bianca*, or "white polenta." Once the more popular crop, it took a back seat to the more resilient yellow varieties. I love *polenta bianca* for its whiff of jasmine, its deep and nuanced sweetness, for the way it seamlessly finds its way down the tongue, all while keeping its structure and bite. But I love it most for being the soulmate to small fish preparations and salt cod. The literal gem among white polenta is Biancoperla (White Pearl), an earlyish twentieth-century hybrid that fell out of favor with the advent of more robust and

cheaper corn. Today Biancoperla, so-called for its opalescence, is still stubbornly and reverently cultivated in the provinces of Padua and Treviso in Veneto.

Another kid on the polenta block is *taragna*, a mix of yellow corn and buckwheat typical of the Valtellina, a region in northeastern Lombardy. Once a hyperlocal specialty, *polenta taragna* has been gaining momentum on the world scene for some time now. It is a definite winter choice, whose best end is met with strong dairy flavors—like parmigiano and cave-aged cheeses—or with woodsy and ashy flavors, like truffle, mushrooms, and root vegetables.

In the United States, polenta has gained a well-established place under the culinary sun, which keeps growing as we become increasingly aware of gluten sensitivities but still crave our carbs. Yet many groan at the time and attention cooking polenta needs. Well, it doesn't. First of all, if you are in a pinch, use *precotta* or even *istantanea*. If you would rather have the full depth of slow-cooking polenta but do not want to be stirring for forty-five minutes or more, follow the double-boiler method that opens this chapter and let polenta become a mainstay in your diet.

I switched to this well-documented method several years ago, after an exploding air bubble in the polenta I was meticulously stirring for a party burned my hand badly enough that I had to recuse myself from the rest of the evening. In addition to improving safety, double-boiler polenta is a largely unattended method. The active time to get it going is less than five minutes, and though the cooking requires about an hour, you will only lift the lid once to give the polenta a quick stir and check the density. All the while your attention can be turned to activities much merrier than stirring away by a hot stove.

The texture and consistency of polenta are the subjects of culture wars. Many prefer a polenta that will fall into one block dense enough to be sliced with a thread. Some prefer a polenta that leaves its cooking vessel in waves. My take is that the main driver of choice should be the cook's preference closely followed by the application. Whatever you do, always make sure to round up the quantity when you make polenta so you will have leftovers to turn into exciting new dishes.

Polenta cotta a bagnomaria
Double-boiler method for cooking polenta

Select a heatproof bowl that sits snugly in the rim of one of your pots. Fill the pot with enough water to touch the bottom of the bowl and set the pot on the stove.

Fill the bowl with 4 cups / 950 ml water and pour in the polenta. Add 1½ teaspoons salt and stir until well blended. Rest the bowl in the pot and cover it with a tight-fitting lid. Turn the heat on to medium-low. Set a timer for 30 minutes. Cook, adjusting the heat if necessary to make sure the water in the pot doesn't boil over.

When the timer goes off, lift the lid and check the thickness of the polenta, adding water if you would like a runnier texture. Whisk, put the lid back, and cook for another 15 to 20 minutes.

Taste to ensure the polenta is well cooked: it should be tender with some textural variations and without lingering raw cereal flavor. Forty-five minutes is usually enough time, though coarser grinds and whole-grain polenta might need a little longer. When it is ready, stir in the butter, taste, and adjust salt and pepper to best suit your palate. Your polenta is ready.

FOR 4 TO 6 PEOPLE

1 cup / 125 g polenta

Salt and pepper

2 to 3 tablespoons unsalted butter (or olive oil for a vegan version)

This morning bowl weaves the Anglo taste for warm morning cereal I have acquired in my adopted country with an ingredient seminal to my place of birth and fluffs it with scents discovered via my half-Egyptian mother-in-law. Whole milk makes this porridge the creamiest, but you lighten the milk with water, or turn to your nondairy milk of choice for a vegan version.

Porridge dolce di polenta bianca
Sweet white polenta porridge

FOR 2 PEOPLE

1 cup / 240 ml whole milk

¼ cup / 30 g white polenta

¼ teaspoon salt

1 teaspoon rose water

2 tablespoons
brown sugar

1½ tablespoons
raw pistachios

A few rose petals

Cook the polenta as described in the double-boiler method (page 103), using the whole milk in place of the water in the top bowl.

When the polenta is ready, stir in the rose water. Spoon into warm bowls, sprinkle with the sugar, and dust with the pistachios. Garnish with the rose petals and serve warm.

I never had a key to the front door of the house where I grew up. There was always someone there to open it. Of what went into feeding a household that, counting family members, staff, and visitors, averaged fifteen people, I understood little. On our never-ending table, anything remaining from a meal became the base for a whole new dish. To this day, leftovers are ingredients in my kitchen: a green soup becomes a sauce for gnocchi, a roast lives on in meatballs, stale bread crunches in a salad.

This casserole is so good and fast to assemble that I cook extra polenta just to have leftovers to make it. This version is a basic one, so feel free to spin it into your own: use a meat sauce instead of plain tomato, add some prosciutto or mushrooms, or go from red to white with Gorgonzola and walnuts.

Polenta di rimedio gratinata
Upcycled baked polenta

Heat the oven to 375°F / 190°C / gas mark 5. Grease a medium-size baking dish with 2 tablespoons of the butter, then coat with 2 tablespoons of the parmigiano.

Slice the polenta and arrange half of the slices in the baking dish. Follow with 1 cup / 240 of the tomato sauce, ¾ cup / 90 g of the shredded cheese, and 2 tablespoons of the parmigiano.

Cover with the remaining polenta slices and then top with the remaining tomato sauce and shredded cheese. Sprinkle with the last of the parmigiano and dot with the remaining 2 tablespoons butter.

Bake for 20 to 25 minutes, just enough to heat thoroughly and melt the cheese into threads. Serve hot.

FOR 6 PEOPLE

4 tablespoons / 60 g unsalted butter

½ cup /120 ml grated parmigiano reggiano

2 cups / 500 g cooked polenta

1½ cups / 350 ml homemade tomato sauce

1 cup / 120 g shredded melty cheese (any kind you like)

The sweetness of white polenta makes it particularly suited to decisively flavored fish of all kinds. Indeed, the cuisine of Veneto has many pairings of fish and white polenta, including this one from Venice, in which small, tentacled sea creatures are stewed in their own ink and served over runny, white polenta. The recipe calls for baby octopuses, which you can buy already cleaned and flash frozen from Asian fishmongers and grocery stores. But any kind of small tentacled creature will do. If you are cleaning the cephalopods yourself and are lucky enough to find the ink sac, pierce it to retrieve the ink. Otherwise, check with local fishmongers or online for squid ink. By the way, if you do clean the octopuses yourself, buy 2 pounds / 1 kg, as weight is lost during cleaning. A disclaimer: As is always the case with specifically territorial dishes, there are thousands of versions, all deliciously definitive. This is mine.

Polipetti al nero con polenta bianca
Baby octopus in squid ink with white polenta

FOR 4 PEOPLE

1 cup / 125 g white polenta

Salt and pepper

½ small yellow onion

1 handful parsley leaves

1½ teaspoons tomato concentrate (or paste)

3 tablespoons extra-virgin olive oil

1½ pounds / 680 g cleaned baby octopuses, thawed if frozen

1 cup / 240 ml dry white wine

1 tablespoon squid ink

Cook the polenta as described in the double-boiler method (page00), using 4 cups / 950 ml water and 1½ teaspoons salt.

Mince the onion. Finely chop the parsley leaves. Dilute the tomato concentrate in 1 cup / 240 ml warm water.

Pour the olive oil into a sauté pan over medium-low heat. When the oil's fragrance wafts effortlessly to your nose, add the onion, one-third of the parsley, and ½ teaspoon salt. Cook, stirring often, for 7 to 8 minutes, until the onion is soft and hazy.

Turn the heat to high and add the octopuses. Sauté just until their color changes to pink. Douse with the wine. When the wine has lost its initial punchiness to the nose and its fumes are sweet and caressing the eyes, stir in the diluted tomato concentrate and the ink.

Lower the heat to medium and cook until the octopuses are tender; depending on their size, they can take anywhere from 10 to 25 minutes. For longer cooking times, you might need to add some warm water. Taste and adjust salt and pepper to please your palate.

When the polenta is ready, sample it and adjust salt and pepper to suit your taste. Pour it into a warm shallow serving bowl, top it with the octopuses, and sprinkle it with the remaining parsley. Serve hot.

A yellow blob of polenta steaming on a marble board, my four siblings and I, forks in hand, fidgeting with hunger; our nanny going around the table ladling the braised pork we'd been smelling for hours, all of our forks working their way toward the center of the same edible plate. Today, my memory of polenta would need a negative COVID test. I still make this dish, which is for togetherness, for the clacking of chatter and the warmth of family and friends. And everyone gets their own plate.

Polenta integrale con spuntature in umido
Whole-grain polenta with braised baby back ribs

Place the sausages and ribs on the counter to come to room temperature. Season the ribs with 1½ teaspoons salt.

Mince the carrots, onion, and celery. If you are pressed for time, you can do this in a food processor. Bundle the bay leaves, herb sprigs, and orange peel strips and secure them with kitchen twine.

Pour the tomatoes into a bowl. Fill the empty can half full with water, swirl and add it to the tomatoes, then squash them with your hands or a potato masher.

Coat the bottom of a wide shallow pot with oil and heat on medium until hovering a hand over it feels uncomfortable. Add the sausages and brown until lightly golden, turning them only when they easily release from the pan. Transfer them to a sheet pan. Do the same with the ribs.

Add the carrots, onion, celery, and herb bundle to the pot along with a generous pinch of salt. Cook over medium heat for about 10 minutes, until the vegetables are hazy, tender, and very fragrant, stirring often to prevent sticking and adding a little warm water if necessary.

Return the sausages and ribs to the pot and stir everything for 1 minute. Raise the heat to high, douse with the wine, and scrape up the caramelization from the bottom of the pan. When the wine has lost its punch and its fumes are sweet, add the tomatoes. When they come to a boil, turn down the heat to low, cover the pot, and simmer for 1 hour, until the meat is fork-tender and the sauce has a soulful, coppery color. Taste and adjust salt and red chili flakes to suit your palate.

Cook the polenta as described in the double-boiler method (page 103), doubling the water and salt, then pour it into a warm serving bowl. Serve the meat on the side. Pass the pecorino at the table for those eaters who would like some.

FOR 8 PEOPLE

8 sweet Italian
sausage links

16 baby back pork ribs,
sliced apart

Salt

2 carrots

1 small yellow onion

1 celery rib

2 bay leaves

1 thyme sprig

1 rosemary sprig

2 long orange peel strips,
each 2 inches / 5 cm wide

1 can (32 ounces / 910 g)
peeled whole tomatoes

3 tablespoons extra-virgin
olive oil

1 cup / 240 ml
dry red wine

Pinch of red chili flakes

2 cups / 250 g
whole-grain polenta

Grated pecorino romano,
for serving

These gnocchi are my adaptation of the classic semolina gnocchi from Rome. Because polenta needs a longer cooking time than semolina, I resort to my tried-and-true double-boiler method. You can bring even more flavor to this dish by adding bits of ham or mushrooms or crumbles of blue cheese. Regular yellow polenta can be substituted for the buckwheat-corn mix.

Gnocchi di polenta taragna al burro nocciola, grana e salvia
Buckwheat polenta with hazelnut butter and chestnuts

Cook the polenta as described in the double-boiler method (page 103), using the whole milk in place of the water in the top bowl and 2 teaspoons salt.

Grease a medium-size shallow baking dish with 1 tablespoon of the butter, then coat with 2 tablespoons of the parmigiano.

Melt 4 tablespoons / 60 g of the butter in a small saucepan with the sage leaves on as low a setting as your stove top allows. After about 20 minutes, the butter will divide into cloudy solids and a golden yellow liquid. Continue cooking for another 20 minutes to caramelize the solids and confit the sage until crinkly.

When the timer goes off, stir the polenta and taste for doneness. If needed, cook longer until the various elements are uniformly soft even though differently ground.

Take the polenta off the heat and add 2 tablespoons of the butter and 4 tablespoons / 60 ml of the parmigiano. Grate nutmeg into the bowl until you smell it without bending down. Stir well and taste the mixture. Adjust salt and pepper to suit your palate. Lastly, vigorously and quickly whisk in the eggs and egg yolk.

Heat the oven to 350°F / 180°C / gas mark 4.

FOR 6 PEOPLE

1 cup / 125 g polenta taragna

4 cups / 950 ml whole milk

Salt and pepper

1 stick / 4 ounces / 115 g unsalted butter

½ cup / 120 ml grated parmigiano reggiano

18 to 24 small and medium sage leaves

Nutmeg, for grating

2 eggs

1 egg yolk

continued

Dampen a cool surface—marble, stainless steel, or a chilled sheet pan. Pour the polenta onto the damp surface and level it to ½-inch / 12-mm thickness with the help of a dampened offset spatula or dinner knife.

Wet a piece of parchment paper large enough to cover the gnocchi dough, squeeze it to remove excess moisture. Lay the paper over the gnocchi, and gently smooth it to adhere and protect the surface from drying and cracking. When the dough is cool enough to touch comfortably, peel off the parchment.

Use a 2-inch / 5-cm square cookie cutter to cut the polenta mixture into equal pieces. Re-spread the leftover mixture and cut out more squares. If you lack a square cutter, use another shape, or simply divide the polenta into 2-inch /5-cm squares with a greased knife.

Arrange the pieces in the prepared baking dish, overlapping them slightly. Dot the top with the remaining 1 tablespoon butter. Cover with aluminum foil and bake for about 15 minutes, removing the foil for the last 5 minutes.

Douse the gnocchi with the warm melted butter and crinkly sage, sprinkle with the remaining 2 tablespoons parmigiano, and serve right away.

This tart is a fall-into-winter pleasure particularly suited for afternoon tea with a spoonful of clotted cream or crème fraîche. Because the timing and texture of quick-cooking polenta differs from brand to brand, you may need to adjust the milk to get to the correct density. If amaretti aren't available, flavor the custard with 1 teaspoon almond extract and add some chopped almonds for texture. Make your life easier by using a tart pan with a removable bottom, if you have one. It makes unmolding the crostata a cinch.

Crostata di crema di polenta con pere e amaretti
Polenta custard tart with pears and amaretti

Make the pasta frolla dough as directed on pages 179–181, then roll out and line a 9- to 10-inch / 23- to 25-cm tart pan with a removable bottom. Refrigerate until needed.

Whisk the egg yolks and sugar together in a bowl until pale yellow and a little fluffy, with well-defined bubbles forming on the surface. Transfer the mixture to a saucepan, then sprinkle in the polenta, letting it fall between your fingers while stirring it in with a wooden spoon.

Pour the milk into a saucepan and heat over medium heat to just below boiling. Transfer the milk to a heatproof measuring pitcher. Set the saucepan with the polenta-egg mixture over medium heat and slowly stream in 2 cups / 475 ml of the hot milk while whisking continuously. Once the milk is in, continue whisking for about 5 minutes, until the polenta is fully cooked. Gauge the consistency: It should be dense but smooth and easy to whisk. If it isn't, whisk in as much additional hot milk as necessary to achieve the right texture.

Turn off the heat, transfer the polenta custard to a cold bowl, and set it aside to cool completely.

Position a rack in the lower third of the oven and a second one in the middle of the oven. Heat the oven to 375°F / 190°C / gas mark 5.

Cut each pear into quarters, then remove the core and stem. Slice each quarter into 4 slices. Crumble the amaretti coarsely. Use three-fourths of them to dust the bottom of the tart shell.

continued

FOR A 9- TO 10-INCH / 23- TO 25-CM TART PAN; FOR 6 TO 8 PEOPLE

Pasta frolla dough for one 10-inch / 25-cm tart shell (page 179)

4 egg yolks

¼ cup / 50 g sugar

¼ cup / 30 g quick-cooking polenta

2 to 3 cups / 475 to 700 ml whole milk

2 ripe but firm pears (Boscs are ideal)

12 amaretti

Crostata di crema di polenta con pere e amaretti, continued

Pour the polenta custard over the amaretti and level it with a dampened offset spatula or dinner knife. Arrange the pear slices over the custard in concentric circles, leaving an empty circle in the center. Mound the remaining amaretti in the center circle.

Place the tart on a sheet pan, loosely tent it with aluminum foil, and slide it onto the rack in the lower third of the oven. Set a timer for 30 minutes. When it goes off, remove the foil and move the tart to the middle rack.

Set the timer for an additional 15 minutes, at the end of which you will test if the tart is done by touching its center; it should softly bounce but not jiggle. If the center still gives a little too much, return the tart to the oven for another 5 to 10 minutes, until it passes the bouncy versus jiggly test.

Remove the tart from the sheet pan and leave it just until the pan is cool enough to handle comfortably. Lift the tart from the outer pan ring and slide it from the bottom circle onto a plate large enough to contain it within its rim. Serve at room temperature.

Insalata di farro estiva
Summer farro salad

Spaghetti al farro primavera con asparagi e piselli
Spring farro spaghetti with asparagus and peas

Zuppa di farro, carciofi e cardoncelli
Farro, artichokes, and king trumpets soup

Minestra di farro spezzato con granchio e castagne
Cracked farro soup with crab and chestnuts

Quaglie ripiene di farro e porcini con sugo di finferli e castagne
Farro and porcini-filled quails with chanterelles and chestnut sauce

Torta di mandorle, farro e pesche
Almond, farro, and peach cake

CHAPTER 6

FARRO / EINKORN, EMMER, & SPELT

The rebirth of an heirloom antique

My brother's 1990 wedding was a four-hundred-plus people affair on our family's ancestral lands along the banks of Umbria's Lake Trasimeno. The to-do was fraught with family tensions exacerbated by unassigned seating and an unexpected wave of humid heat. But then the barely warm farro soup laden with thirst-quenching vegetables and cooling herbs was served. It was a humble showstopper that reminded us how much more there was to bring us together than to tear us apart. That was the day when this grain, which had been part of background food chatter my whole life, reified in the language of my own cooking. I remember bringing a few bags with me to the States, as back then, the rebirth of this heirloom antique was well on its way in Italy but still in its predawn in the United States.

Farro was the first domesticated wheat, likely by the Egyptians. People all around the Mediterranean basin and in northern Europe ground it into flour for millennia. It was a well-documented staple in the diet of the Etruscans of central Italy and is said to have sustained Roman legions in war. We can think of it as the OG wheat—*triticum* in Latin. With agricultural leaps, farro was almost entirely supplanted by kinds of wheat with denser yield and higher protein content. But in the last few decades, dedicated farmers have rediscovered the ancient grain and brought it to the attention of chefs and cooks who are folding it into their cooking in new, inventive ways.

Three different grains fall into what today is sold as farro: einkorn, emmer, and spelt. They are united by their resistance to free threshing, or in plain terms, the bran stays tightly put around the kernels during threshing. Therefore, farro needs further processing to release the grains. This common peculiarity is what most explains farro's higher price compared with other types of wheat or wheat-adjacent cereals.

The most visible difference among these three siblings in arms is size, starting from *farro piccolo* (einkorn), on to *farro medio* (emmer), and finally to *farro grande* (spelt). Beyond size, there are subtle agricultural differences and cleaning-process variations that impact farro's flavor profile and culinary use.

Farro piccolo or einkorn—botanically *Triticum monococcum*—is reputed to have the highest density of nutrients. It has a pronounced and long-lasting flavor of ash and minerals. Rows of individually wrapped grains alternate in a flat row with long spikelets. Although the baby in size, it is considered the most ancient. As a whole berry, it commands a premium, and ground into flour, it is prized for specialty bread making. It is well suited for soups and salads.

Farro medio or emmer—botanically *Triticum dicoccum*—has two large grains in each bran pocket and slightly shorter, irregularly placed spikelets. Its flavor moves toward delicate smoke and toasted pine nut. Because of a yield higher than *farro piccolo*, and a long shelf life, farro medio is the most commonly commercialized. Indeed, if the bag is simply marked farro, it is surely *farro medio*. This jack-of-all-trades works across preparations calling for the ingredient.

Farro grande or spelt—botanically *Triticum spelta*—can have up to three very large grains growing in one sac. Its spikelets are shorter and softer than in *piccolo* and *medio*, and its color can veer to pink when mature. It is close to soft summer wheat; its gluten content is a little higher than that of its siblings, and its flavor more delicate and shallower. *Farro grande* is generally used as flour or made into *farro spezzato*, a cracked version of this cereal suited for an unusual morning bowl or for a last-minute addition to a soup.

Farro kernels can be processed in three different ways, determined by how much of the bran is removed. The method affects the cooking time and the mouthfeel. Choose it according to your preference and the grain's intended use.

Integrale (whole grain) denotes that the farro was merely cleaned from debris and its bran left intact. Whole-grain farro is nutty brown with matte grains. I always give it a once over since I almost broke a tooth on a left-behind stone in 1996. A night of rest in water plumps the kernels and shortens the cooking. It is chewy and a little bouncy. I love it for salads.

Semiperlato (semi-scrubbed or semi-pearled) means the chaff was partially scrubbed off. The grains look dusty with hazelnut brown and off-white spots. It does not need to be soaked and will cook in about a half hour. Semi-pearled farro offers the best balance between the grain's characteristic flavor and a friendly texture.

Perlato (scrubbed or pearled) is farro whose bran has been completely removed. It requires only about fifteen minutes of boiling and gets mushy when overcooked. *Perlato* releases a greater amount of starch than its fellow farro kin. It is best for soups and for preparations that benefit from the gossamer that spins when starch acts as the matchmaker between water and fat.

Farro can also be ground into flour, or cracked into *farro spezzato*—cracked farro, an uneven coarse porridge—that can be cooked into a warm breakfast, added to a winter soup, or even take the place of polenta.

The most prized farro crops are from the Tuscan region of Garfagnana near Lucca, and from the valleys around Monteleone di Spoleto in Umbria. They boast an PGI and PDO seal of quality, respectively, and because their productions are limited, they aren't easy to find. If you do happen to run across them, I cannot recommend them enough.

While farro's flavor profile is especially suited to the autumnal culinary basket of mushrooms and chestnuts, it can also have a place in the scented breeze of spring and the sunshine of summer. As a minimally processed grain, farro can go stale if it sits on a shelf too long, so no matter when and how you use it, always smell it first. It should have a dusty aroma with hints of woods and fresh nuts. If it smells old and rancid, toss it into the compost.

This salad is farro's claim to a place in the summer sun. My friend and former business partner, Yolanda Garretti, and I conceived it during our catering days as an alternative to pasta salad on summer buffets. Farro kernels keep their bite and gloss longer and better than even the hardiest pasta shape. The version here is vegan, but for a one-bowl lunch, you can finish it with a smattering of crumbled feta or top it with a couple of sardines.

Insalata di farro estiva
Summer farro salad

Fill a saucepan with 2 quarts / 2 L water and set it over heat to come to a boil.

While the water is coming to a boil, place the farro in a colander, pick it over, and rinse it.

Season the boiling water with 1 tablespoon salt and pour the farro into it. Adjust the heat so the water keeps a medium boil and cook for 20 to 25 minutes, until the farro is tender but with a firm bite.

In the meantime, prepare the rest of the ingredients. Pit the olives, rinse them well to eliminate the brine, and leave them to soak in warm water. Wash all visible salt off the capers and leave them soaking in warm water.

Cut the cherry tomatoes into quarters and place them in a colander resting over a bowl. Season with 1 teaspoon salt, the oregano, and pepper to taste. Toss well and leave undisturbed to lose some moisture.

Stack the basil leaves, roll them up tightly lengthwise, and slice them crosswise into thin ribbons.

When the farro is ready, drain it into a colander and rinse it under cold water. Shake off the excess water well and pour it into a bowl. Drain the capers and olives and add them to the farro, then add the tomatoes and half of the basil. Toss well and sample. Add salt and pepper to best suite your taste and toss again.

Squeeze the lemon half over the farro and tomatoes and toss. Lastly, douse with 2 to 3 tablespoons olive oil and toss again. Taste a spoonful and, if necessary, adjust the balance of lemon, olive oil, salt, and pepper to best suit your palate.

Garnish with the remaining basil and enjoy the salad from cool to room temperature.

FOR 5 TO 6 PEOPLE

1 cup / 170 g semi-pearled farro

Salt and pepper

2 tablespoons black olives

2 tablespoons capers packed in salt

1 cup / 150 g cherry tomatoes

1 teaspoon dried oregano

1 cup / 40 g packed basil leaves

½ lemon

Extra-virgin olive oil as needed

It's not easy being pasta. Your outer layer must budge to every bite, but your core can never capitulate. Your job is to be the ideal complement, yet no one will choose you if you cannot stand on your own. And then there is *pasta al farro*. One does not stumble upon *pasta al farro*; rather, one seeks its viscous coating, woodsy interior, and determined taste, one bows to its demand for a simple sauce that happily plays second fiddle. It was spring when this dish was inspiredly portrayed by my photographer Molly's hand. Asparagus and sugar snap peas were a natural fit. But if you make this recipe yours, any season can gift the right vegetable.

Spaghetti al farro primavera con asparagi e piselli
Spring farro spaghetti with asparagus and peas

FOR 6 PEOPLE

1 bunch asparagus

8 ounces / 225 g sugar snap peas

1 small shallot

3 tablespoons extra-virgin olive oil, plus more for finishing

Salt and pepper

1 package (1 pound / 450 g) farro spaghetti

Grated parmigiano reggiano or pecorino romano, for serving

Fill a tall pot with 4 quarts / 4 L water, cover it, and set it over heat to come to a boil.

Hold an asparagus by the tip and run your thumb and index finger along the stem, gently pressing up with the thumb, until you find the spot that yields enough for the bottom to snap. Don't force it; let the asparagus tell you where that spot is. Repeat until all the asparagus bottoms are snapped off. Slice the asparagus into wheels ¼ inch / 6 mm thick, leaving the tips whole.

Snap any stems off the sugar snap peas, then cut all the peas at a slant into 3 pieces each. Grate the shallot on the second smallest holes of a box grater.

Pour the oil into a large frying pan over medium-low heat and stand by the stove until the oil's fragrance wafts up to your nostrils. Stir in the shallot with 1 teaspoon salt and let it sizzle gently, stirring occasionally, for about 3 minutes, until it is glassy and hazy.

The water should be boiling by now. Season it with 1 tablespoon salt, drop in the spaghetti, stir, and cover the pot. Set a timer for 3 minutes shy of the suggested cooking time. When the water starts to boil again, remove the cover and adjust the heat so the water is at a lively, but not rolling, boil.

Add the asparagus and sugar snaps to the frying pan and raise the heat to medium-high. Cook, stirring often to prevent the shallot from burning and the asparagus and peas from sticking, for 5 to 7 minutes, until the vegetables are tender. Taste and adjust salt and pepper to suit your palate.

continued

Spaghetti al farro primavera con asparagi e piselli, continued

When the timer goes off, fish the spaghetti out of the water with tongs and add them to the frying pan. Raise the heat to high and douse the spaghetti with ½ cup / 120 ml of the pasta cooking water. Swirl the pan to swish the pasta around while it continues to absorb water and mosey on toward cooking completion. It will take 2 to 3 minutes, during which you will need to add a little more pasta cooking water. Do so in small amounts. The starch in the water and the fat in the sauce will bind all along the spaghetti into a gossamer of flavors.

Transfer to a platter, finish with a thread of olive oil, and serve right away with some cheese on the side for those who might want it.

This is the first of two recipes in this chapter featuring farro with mushrooms. These two ingredients join in a canvas that spins charming tableaus across space and time. We are in mid to late spring with this soup, originating from a version that was part of my brother's wedding buffet in 1990. Oyster and king trumpet mushrooms are abundant, while artichokes are at their tail end, too tough for salads and steaming but still well suited for longer cooking preparations. Green garlic completes the seasonal picture. A pearled farro is the best choice for this dish. If you cannot find green garlic, use a clove or two of regular garlic or a small shallot.

Zuppa di farro, carciofi e cardoncelli
Farro, artichokes, and king trumpets soup

Cut the lemon in half and squeeze the juice into a bowl of cold water. Drop the squeezed lemon halves into the water.

Pick up the first artichoke and remove the outer leaves until about two-thirds of the outer circle of leaves are a lighter, somewhat yellowish green. Slice off the darker tips of the leaves close to the top, being mindful of the thorns. Pare the outer part of the bottom and peel the stem. Finally, slice off a very thin layer from the bottom of the stem. This procedure is called turning, as for each phase of it, your knife will circle around the artichoke.

Cut the turned artichoke in half lengthwise and remove the choke if necessary. The choke is that hay-like fuzz that is often, but not always, in the middle of an artichoke. Thinly slice each half lengthwise and drop them into the lemon water to prevent oxidation. Perform the turning procedure on all the remaining artichokes. Rub your hands and fingers all over with the lemon halves to remove the bitterness. Wash them well with soap and water. Do not forgo this last step, lest the bitter residue travels to other ingredients your hands will touch.

FOR 4 PEOPLE

1 lemon

6 medium-size artichokes, or 12 to 15 baby ones

1 pound / 450 g king trumpet or oyster mushrooms

1 green garlic stalk (see headnote for substitution)

Salt and pepper

2 strips marjoram

1 cup / 170 g semi-pearled farro

2 tablespoons extra-virgin olive oil, plus more for finishing

1 cup / 240 ml dry white wine

Grated aged pecorino, for serving

continued

Zuppa di farro, carciofi e cardoncelli, continued

Wipe the mushrooms clean with a paper towel, trim the very bottom of the stems, and slice them thinly. Clean the green garlic much like you would a scallion: trim off the bottom hairy root and the top third of the green leaves and remove the outer layer. Mince the cleaned garlic into a paste with 1 teaspoon salt. Strip the marjoram leaves and chop them finely. Place the farro in a colander, pick it over, and rinse it.

Pour the olive oil into a saucepan with the green garlic and half of the marjoram. Set over medium-low heat and stand by the stove to closely tend to the garlic and prevent it from burning. Drain the artichokes and shake off the excess moisture.

In 3 to 4 minutes, when the garlic looks hazy and its fragrance is intoxicating, add the sliced artichokes and mushrooms and mix well. When the mushrooms begin to sweat and wilt, stir in the farro then raise the heat to medium-high. Douse with the wine. Wait until the wine's alcoholic punch to your nose has turned into a sugary caress to your eyes. Cover abundantly with warm water and bring to a boil.

Lower the heat until the soup is at a simmer. Sample a spoonful of the liquid and adjust the salt to suit your taste. Cover and simmer for 20 to 30 minutes, until the farro is quite tender and the vegetables are well cooked. You may need to add more warm water along the way.

This is a dense and hearty soup. If you prefer soupier soups, you can accentuate its brothiness with some warm water. Just remember to rebalance the seasoning that may have gotten diluted in plain water.

Serve warm, finished with a thread of olive oil and dusted with the remaining marjoram. Offer the pecorino at the table for those eaters who would like some.

My culture—Umbrian farro—and my identity—Bay Area Dungeness crab—
come together in this soup that I created a few years back for my teaching
curriculum. It is one of the dishes of which I am proudest and has become
an expected feature on my family's Thanksgiving table. Dungeness crab has
a limited season, local to the San Francisco Bay Area, but you can substitute
with shrimp or any crab available where you live. If you cannot find cracked
farro, use any whole kernel farro and adjust the cooking time by consulting
the instructions on the package. Precooked vacuum-packed chestnuts are
a tasty snack and a great shortcut for this recipe. For a gluten-free version,
make this soup with cannellini beans or chickpeas.

Minestra di farro spezzato con granchio e castagne
Cracked farro soup with crab and chestnuts

FOR 6 TO 8 PEOPLE

1 medium-size Dungeness
crab, cooked and cracked

1 small yellow onion

5 whole cloves

1 carrot

1 celery rib

6 to 8 parsley sprigs

2 bay leaves

2 lemon slices

4 to 5 black peppercorns

Salt and ground pepper

1 large shallot

1½ cups / 170 g cooked and
peeled chestnuts

1½ cups / 255 g cracked farro

2 tablespoons extra-virgin
olive oil, plus more for
finishing (optional)

1 cup / 240 ml dry white wine

Crème fraîche, for serving
(optional)

The first step is picking the crabmeat and making the crab stock, which can
be done up to 2 days in advance.

Pick the crabmeat from both the legs and the body and refrigerate it until
you are ready to use it. Place the empty shells in a stockpot.

Peel the onion, leaving one layer of golden skin on. Spike the onion with
the cloves and drop it into the pot. Crack the carrot and celery in half with
your hands and add them to the pot. Pick the parsley leaves off the stems,
toss the stems into the pot, and save the leaves. Drop the bay leaves, lemon
slices, peppercorns, and 1½ tablespoons salt into the stockpot, then fill it
with 3 quarts / 3 L water.

Place the pot on the stove over heat, and as soon as the liquid comes to
a boil, lower the heat until it is at a gentle simmer. Skim the surface with a
spoon to remove any scum, then simmer, uncovered, for about 2 hours.
Transfer the stock to a cool container and refrigerate as is; you will strain
it when ready to use.

When ready to make the soup, strain the stock into a saucepan and bring it
to a boil. Then cover it and keep it on the lowest heat setting to keep warm.

Grate the shallot on the second smallest holes of a box grater. Finely chop
the parsley leaves. Roughly chop the chestnuts. Rinse the cracked farro in
a tight-mesh colander.

Pour the olive oil into a large saucepan and set it over very low heat. When you can detect its fragrance without bending over the stove, add the shallot, half of the parsley, and a pinch of salt. Cook, stirring occasionally, for 3 to 4 minutes, until the shallot is quite fragrant and beginning to turn a little golden. Add the chestnuts and farro, then stir well for a couple of minutes to coat them in shallot deliciousness. Raise the heat to high and douse with the wine.

When the wine no longer punches your nose with acidity but sweetly caresses your eyes, pour the hot stock over the chestnuts and farro, lower the heat, and simmer until the farro is cooked. It should take about 15 minutes, but check it at 10 minutes to be sure it is not becoming too mushy. Sample a spoonful and adjust the seasoning with salt and pepper to suit your taste.

Warm six bowls and scatter an equal amount of the crabmeat on the bottom of each one. Ladle the hot soup on top, garnish with the remaining parsley, and drizzle with a little crème fraîche before serving. If you prefer to stay away from dairy, finish with a thread of olive oil.

Mushrooms appear again in this recipe, paired with another ingredient we all need to embrace out of the Valhalla of rarefied, challenging ingredients to which it's been unjustly relegated: quail. The flavor of quail is distinct but not gamy, and the meat is dense but not stringy. Quail cook quickly, and it takes more skill to mess them up than it does to nail them. And if the price was ever a factor, look again: quail can be sourced for as little as $2.50 a bird, less than the average for one pound (450 grams) of organic chicken breast. If you can plan ahead, brining will give the quail a velvetier mouthfeel and reduce the already short cooking time, but you can skip the step and still have on-point results. One more tip: if you are looking to impress, shave some black truffle over the quail right before bringing them to the table.

Quaglie ripiene di farro e porcini con sugo di finferli e castagne
Farro and porcini–filled quail with chanterelles and chestnut sauce

To brine the quail, dissolve the kosher salt in 1 cup /240 ml hot water and then mix it with 1 quart / 1 L cold water. Place the quail in a 2-quart / 2-l container and pour the salted water over them. Cover the container and leave the quail to brine in the refrigerator for 2 to 3 hours. Drain the tiny birds and dry them well inside and out. Lay them on a sheet pan and refrigerate uncovered for 1 hour.

While the quail are brining, make the filling. Fill a 2-cup / 475-ml measuring pitcher with hot water and drown the porcini in it. Leave them soaking so that they plump and soften.

Fill a saucepan with 1 quart / 1 L water and set it over heat to come to a boil. Drop the farro into a colander, pick it over, and rinse it. When the water is boiling, season it with 1 teaspoon salt and stir in the farro. Lower the heat until the water is at a gentle boil and cook the farro for about 20 minutes, until quite tender but with structure. Drain it as soon as it is ready so it doesn't overcook.

FOR 4 PEOPLE

To brine the quail
¼ cup / 35 g kosher salt

4 quail

For the filling
1 ounce / 30 g dried porcini

Salt and pepper

½ cup / 85 g semi-pearled farro

1 shallot

1 lemon

¼ cup / 5 g loosely packed parsley leaves

continued

2 tablespoons
extra-virgin olive oil

½ cup / 120 ml
dry white wine

Nutmeg, for grating

For the sauce and quail
1 shallot

6 thyme sprigs

1 pound / 450 g
chanterelle mushrooms

1 cup / 115 g cooked and
peeled chestnuts

Salt and pepper

3 tablespoons
extra-virgin olive oil

1 cup / 240 ml
brandy or Cognac

1 cup / 240 ml
chicken stock

Meanwhile, grate the shallot on the second smallest holes of a box grater. Grate 2 teaspoons zest from the lemon. Finely chop the parsley.

Drain the porcini, collecting their soaking liquid in a bowl. Rinse and chop the mushrooms. Filter the soaking liquid through a tight-mesh strainer to remove any grit. Reserve.

Pour the olive oil into a frying pan and set it over low heat. When you can detect its fragrance without bending over the stove, add the shallot and 1 teaspoon salt. Cook, stirring occasionally, for 3 to 4 minutes, until the shallot is quite fragrant and hazy and beginning to turn a little golden. Add the porcini, parsley, and lemon zest, raise the heat to medium, and stir for 2 minutes.

Douse the mushrooms with the wine, and when the acidic fumes of the wine's alcohol have been replaced by the sweet caress of its sugar, add 1 cup / 240 ml of the porcini soaking liquid. Turn the heat down to medium-low and cook the porcini, stirring occasionally, for another 8 to 10 minutes, until the liquid has evaporated. Transfer them to a bowl.

Combine the porcini and farro in a bowl and grate nutmeg over them just until you catch a whiff of it without bending over the bowl. Stir the filling well and taste it, then adjust salt and pepper to suit your palate. Spoon the filling into each quail.

Cut a 2-foot / 60-cm length of butcher's twine. Cross the quail's feet and secure them with a knot, leaving all but 2 inches / 5 cm of the twine on one end of the knot. Run the long end of the twine up the quail's tummy to its chest. Pin the string with a finger to the quail's chest and make a 90-degree bend. Run the twine all around the chest, tightening the wings to the body, then loop it under the 90-degree bend. Pull the twine up toward the quail's neck, then down all around the back and the bum to rejoin the short end hanging from the feet. Tie the two ends together and snip off excess twine. Repeat until all 4 quail are trussed into neat packages.

Leave the quail on the counter to come to room temperature while you prepare the ingredients for the sauce.

Slice the shallot paper-thin. Rub the thyme sprigs between your palms to release their fragrance. Free the chanterelles of dirt and other debris with a brush, trim the very bottom of the stems, and then slice them. Roughly chop the chestnuts.

Dry any condensation off the quail if necessary and season them lightly with salt and pepper.

Place a frying pan—preferably a well-seasoned cast-iron one—on medium heat and hover your hand over it until it becomes uncomfortable. Add 2 tablespoons of the olive oil and swirl the pan to distribute it uniformly. Add the quail breast side down and listen for the sizzle that preludes good caramelization. It will take 3 to 4 minutes until the birds' bosoms are browned enough that you can lift them off the pan without having to pull. Turn the quail over and brown their backs and lastly their sides. Transfer them to a plate.

Add the remaining olive oil, the sliced shallot, and the thyme sprigs to the pan and swirl quickly over medium-low heat for 3 to 4 minutes to soften the shallot. Toss in the chanterelles and add 1 teaspoon salt. When the mushrooms start to wilt, add the chestnuts and stir to coat everything in the deliciousness. Cook for about 10 minutes, stirring often. The mushrooms will wilt completely and release some moisture.

Return the quail to the pan and turn the heat to its highest setting. Douse the birds with the brandy. The pan will likely catch fire. Don't fret; just step back and wait for the fire to die down as the alcohol burns off.

Step back up to the stove to pour ½ cup / 120 ml each of the porcini soaking liquid and the stock into the pan. Lower the heat to medium and continue cooking for 8 to 10 minutes, stirring occasionally. The quail will be done by now. Move them to a warm serving platter and cover them with aluminum foil to trap the heat.

Tighten the sauce for another 5 to 8 minutes, until the liquid is slightly viscous and a deep, glossy tobacco brown. Add more stock if you would like a runnier sauce. Sample a spoonful and adjust salt and pepper to suit your palate.

Snip and remove the twine from each bird, then spoon the sauce over the quail. Serve right away.

Farro flour gives this cake the feel of a late-summer twilight—golden, long, and with a whiff of smoke from the cleaning of fields. The only challenging task in this recipe is remembering to leave the butter on the counter to soften until it is like hair pomade. The rest is quite foolproof.

A handheld or stand mixer will speed up creaming the butter and sugar and emulsifying the eggs into the batter for some extra cakey fluff, but gleeful beating by hand also does the job. You can swap out farro for buckwheat flour for a gluten-free version; just add an extra ½ teaspoon baking powder to help with the rising.

Torta di mandorle, farro e pesche
Almond, farro, and peach cake

Line the bottom of a 9- to 10-inch / 23- to 25-cm springform pan with parchment paper. Position a rack in the lower third of the oven and heat the oven to 375°F / 190°C / gas mark 5.

Cream the butter and sugar together with an electric mixer until the sugar has completely dissolved and the mixture looks creamy and homogenous. Whisk in the eggs one at a time, ending with the yolk and making sure to work each egg in completely before adding the next. Stir in the almond extract.

Sift together the farro flour and baking powder into a bowl. Stir in the almond flour and salt. Mix the dry ingredients into the wet ingredients with a rubber spatula until well combined.

Pour the batter into the prepared springform pan and level with an offset spatula or dinner knife. Refrigerate while you prepare the peaches.

Halve the peaches and pry out the pits, then slice each half into 8 wedges. Arrange the wedges in concentric circles on the cake batter, pushing them down slightly. Place the springform pan on a sheet pan.

Bake for 40 to 50 minutes, until a toothpick inserted into the center comes out clean. Let the cake cool for 15 minutes. Run a knife all around the edges then unclasp and lift off the pan sides.

Hold the cake with one hand and with the other pull a corner of the parchment paper and slide it from the pan bottom onto a plate or a cake stand. Cut a slice of the cake and eat it in glee and delight while no one is watching. Let the rest of the cake cool completely and lightly dust the top with confectioners' sugar using a tea strainer.

Covered with a clean cloth, this humble delight will last for up to 4 days.

MAKES ONE 9- TO 10-INCH /23- TO 25- CM CAKE; FOR 8 TO 10 PEOPLE

1¾ sticks / 7 ounces / 200 g unsalted butter, softened into a pomade

¾ cup / 150 g granulated sugar

3 eggs

1 egg yolk

1½ teaspoons almond extract or rum (optional)

½ cup / 70 g farro flour

2 teaspoons baking powder

1¾ cups / 150 g almond flour

½ teaspoon salt

2 peaches

Confectioners' sugar, for dusting

LATTICINI / DAIRY

Pesto postumo della mamma
My mother's posthumous pesto

Sablè di parmigiano al pimentòn e mandarino
Tangerine and smoked paprika parmigiano biscuits

Chiocciole al burro e parmigiano aromatiche
Spice-scented butter and parmigiano snail-shell pasta

Calamarata al pecorino e cozze
Calamarata pasta with pecorino and mussels

Sformatini di parmigiano e pistacchi
Parmigiano and pistachio tiny flans

Sformatini di scarola e pinoli al pecorino
Escarole and pine nuts tiny flans with pecorino

Funghi di bosco al cartoccio con pecorino e timo
Wild mushrooms en papillote with pecorino and thyme

CHAPTER 7

PARMIGIANO REGGIANO & PECORINO ROMANO

Ruling the kingdom of cheese side by side

Very little defines Italy to the rest of the world like parmigiano reggiano and pecorino romano. They are symbols of the country's food culture that need neither introduction nor translation. Millennia of craft and wisdom have shaped parmigiano and pecorino into flavors that amplify and ameliorate even the most humble dish. The agricultural, social, and economic impact they have had in their respective territories has been so profound that they are legally protected with a PDO seal.

No Italian has conscious memories of their life before parmigiano reggiano. That's because we Italians have such faith in the miraculous properties of this cheese that we include it among babies' first foods. I still have the twenty-year-old handout from my son's Italian pediatrician with a weaning recipe that includes a homemade vegetable stock, rice cereal, olive oil, and grated parmigiano—and yes, it is quite tasty. As children grow, parmigiano remains their superfood, packed in lunch boxes and handed out by Italian soccer moms all over the world. It can even be found in bar-size packets at vending machines in Italian railway stations.

Parmigiano reggiano is a hard cheese whose history started a thousand years back with Cistercian monks and went on to show the world how agricultural tradition can be scaled while maintaining pristine quality. Today's production pairs more lactiferous cow breeds with regulated nutrition and thermally controlled environments and the sensorial skills of highly trained cheesemakers able to cull peak quality from the interaction between curd and whey.

All phases of parmigiano reggiano production, from feeding and milking the cattle to aging the wheels, happen exclusively in the provinces of Parma, Reggio Emilia, Modena, and Bologna in eastern Emilia-Romagna and Mantua in southern Lombardy, where more than fifty thousand people make close to four million wheels every year. Each wheel requires about 132 gallons (500 liters) of milk. Calf's rennet is added to form a curd, which is then cut into granules as small as rice grains. With skillfully applied heat, the curd coagulates and then precipitates in a mass that, after draining in linen, is cut in half and tightened into its characteristic shape with bands. A small casein plate with a unique QR code is applied to the wheels for full traceability. The tightening bands are pinned with a bas-relief of dots spelling the words parmigiano reggiano all around and with the dairy's identification code and the date of production on one end. Next, the marked wheels are cured in a saturated saline solution and then finally aged in designated, climatized chambers. After twelve months, trained experts examine each wheel and either brand it as parmigiano reggiano or strip it of all distinctive markings and send it to be sold as generic table cheese.

At twelve to nineteen months, parmigiano reggiano has a delicate flavor, with the tang of grass and the sweetness of milk. It has hardly any crystallization, and its buttery character makes it suited for shaving to add a light and fresh note. Drink bubbles with it. Starting at twenty and until twenty-six months, the cheese embarks on the path to harmonious balance that reaches its peak at twenty-four months, at which point parmigiano is crumbly and has visible crystals. The tang gives way to saltiness, and the sensation of butter is still detectable. This is the best parmigiano for grating. It calls for a good white or a light-bodied red. From twenty-seven to thirty-four months, parmigiano is friable and somewhat dry. The crystals are developed enough to variegate the sensations of flavor on the tongue. This parmigiano is more than good grated but may be better enjoyed with some dried fruit and a full-bodied red. Once it goes beyond thirty-five months, parmigiano invades your senses with myriad different sensations. It is like amber to the eyes, fermented hay to the nose. On the tongue, the increased salinity is matched by an intensified sweetness that can carry notes of ripe figs and chocolate. We call this a meditation cheese: pour a glass of your favorite whiskey, sit down, and let this wise cheese carry you away.

On the land next to the olive grove of my childhood home, there lived a flock of sheep whose lives and times are at the root of my pecorino appreciation. The aromas the sheep emanated while grazing among the olive trees changed with the seasons. They were pungent with the cold and grew softer as they neared maternity. The fragrances found life in the cheeses that Remo Vignali, the flock's shepherd, made by hand in the wood fire–heated room below the home he occupied with his wife, Irma, and his daughters, Carla and Maddalena. His skilled hands could make anything from raveggiolo, a glossy, tremulous fresh cheese that tasted like nasturtium and warm milk, to a six-month-old grating pecorino with notes of burnt salted caramel that would send my mother's already remarkable pasta and beans into overdrive.

Many think of pecorino simply as the other grating cheese, but say pecorino to an Italian and you evoke a wide world of flavor and texture sensations. Pecorino is the name given to a wheel of cheese of varying age made with whole sheep's milk ranging in weight from one to eighty pounds (450 grams to 36 kilograms). Excepting the ones that make up the over-the-knee portion of the thigh-high boot, the rest of Italy's regions produce pecorino, including my very own Umbria, where instructions to top a dish with cheese are often understood to mean pecorino. There are hundreds of pecorinos, but one emerges as the undisputed ruler, in both portly size and worldly fame: pecorino romano.

Despite its name, the area of production of pecorino romano extends beyond Lazio—the region of which Rome is a part—to the island of Sardinia and the Tuscan province of Grosseto. Both the milk and lamb's rennet used in its making come from flocks local to the area of transformation. A wheel of pecorino romano is a cylinder whose diameter starts at 10 inches (25 centimeters) and can go up to 15 inches (38 centimeters), with a height spanning 10 to 20 inches (25 to 50 centimeters), for

a total weight ranging between 40 and 80 pounds (18 and 36 kilograms). It starts with raw, filtered sheep's milk heated and coagulated with lamb's rennet. The curd is broken into wheat kernel–size pieces and salted. As the whey cools, the curd forms a mass that is then pressed into wheels. To pass muster, it requires a minimum of five months of aging, at which point it acquires a fresh hay quality with hints of sweet spices that make it an engaging table cheese best paired with honey and fresh fruit. It isn't until it has aged for a full eight months that pecorino romano blossoms into the salt-forward, inimitable grating cheese the world has come to love.

Young pecorino romano mostly stays inside Italy. It is the wheels aged more than eight months that command the premium needed to make export worth the work. When buying pecorino romano, be sure your money goes toward the real deal. On a chunk, look for the imprint of a stylized sheep's head with the words pecorino romano along its ears. If you prefer it grated, look for the PDO red-and-gold seal on the package.

The similarities of parmigiano reggiano and pecorino romano do not extend to flavor. Indeed, their organoleptic characteristics are quite different. Parmigiano slowly shows the wisdom of its old age with subtle, changing notes of ferment, nuts, hay, and chocolate. Pecorino flexes its young muscles with an immediate punch of salt followed shortly by hints of farm grass and yogurt. In the Italian pantry, they rule side by side, skirting each other's boundaries without ever crossing them.

Pesto postumo della mamma
My mother's posthumous pesto

My mother's hands especially mesmerized me when she created her own ever-changing version of pesto with herbs beyond basil and nuts beyond pine. My mother, like her pesto, was made of nonconforming flavors that people did not expect yet talked about for days.

My last memory of my mother's pesto happened after her death. My siblings and I were sorting through her things, longing for a conversation from which she exited way too early. Lunchtime came, and one of us found a jar of pesto in the freezer, labeled and dated in the earlier part of the summer that would be her last. To a person, we each found a task: boiling the water, selecting the pasta, setting the table. We sat and ate, silently wrapped in the love she rarely spoke of but always expressed with her cooking. That meal will forever define the flavor of pesto for me.

My unique version of pesto is based on that memory, but there are a few tenets that hold true across pesto making. I invite you to make them yours. Garlic should not be a defining flavor of pesto, rather a sensation, so don't overdo it. An equal weight of leaves and nuts is a technique I acquired during my own professional growth in the kitchen. I have used it successfully in many a version of pesto. It is important to stir in the cheese by hand after processing, as the blades will clump it into fat globules that can throw off both balance and texture. Pesto should be a thick paste that barely releases oil.

When you are ready to use the pesto, calculate just over ½ cup / 120 g for 1 pound / 450 g of pasta. While the pasta is cooking, drop the pesto into a warm serving bowl. A few minutes before draining the pasta, dilute the pesto with ½ to 1 cup / 120 to 240 ml pasta cooking water.

Store your pesto in a glass jar, topping it with a little olive oil to prevent oxidation. Before putting it away, re-top with a little fresh oil. I keep my pesto in the refrigerator for up to two weeks. My mother used to freeze her pesto in manageable-size jars.

Pesto can complement things other than pasta. In my childhood home, it was a staple on minestrone. It is great with gnocchi, you can use it for a spring lasagna, or spread it on bread. I love it with anchovies, but I love anything with anchovies.

continued

Pesto postumo della mamma, continued

Rinse the basil and parsley leaves carefully with cold water in the basket of a salad spinner. Place the basket in the spinner and spin as you would salad greens. Pour out the water that gathered on the bottom and fluff the leaves. Spin, pour, and fluff again three or four times. Tip the leaves onto a clean cloth and pat dry. Remember that oil and water do not mix, and there is quite a bit of oil in pesto.

Strip the leaves off the marjoram sprigs and add them to the basil and parsley. Weigh all the leaves and then measure an equivalent weight in nuts. You can mix the nuts evenly or have more of one kind or the other. The proportion should be dictated by taste and availability.

Smash and peel the garlic clove. Toss it into the food processor with the nuts and 1 teaspoon salt. Run the processor to give the garlic and nuts a first rough chop.

Stop the processor, add all the herbs, and use a spatula or wooden spoon to push them toward the bottom while also lifting the garlic and nuts to mix everything. Turn the motor back on and, after about 30 seconds, start slowly streaming in olive oil. You will end up using between ½ and ⅔ cup / 120 and 160 ml oil. Keep in mind that pesto should not be floating in oil, so err on the side of less; you can always add more later.

Keep the processor running until you have a fairly dense mixture with very minced leaves. Sample the mixture; if it tastes grassy, continue mincing until it tastes herby and fresh but not grassy. When ready, drag all the pesto into a bowl with a rubber spatula.

Now stir in the cheeses and taste again. Adjust salt and pepper to suit your taste. You may have to add more cheese or salt or pepper. Stir in a few drops of lemon juice.

I should warn you that my mother would denounce the lemon juice as modern treachery, but I find that a few drops bring balance and brightness to the final product, so I've rebelled.

**MAKES ABOUT
2 CUPS / 480 G**

3 cups / 120 g packed basil leaves

1 cup / 20 g loosely packed parsley leaves

6 marjoram sprigs

Raw pine nuts and/or lightly toasted peeled almonds as needed

1 garlic clove

Salt and pepper

Extra-virgin olive oil as needed

2 to 3 tablespoons grated parmigiano reggiano

2 to 3 tablespoons grated pecorino romano

½ lemon

To support her husband's career as a diplomat, my friend Flavia Destefanis's mother became a consummate hostess, renowned for both her infectious laugh and the delectability of her cooking. The base for these savory biscuits comes from her arsenal of surefire aperitivi, and the pimentón (smoked paprika) and zest are my addition. Successful execution of these easy umami bites hinges on one thing: precise weight measures. Cups and spoons, while faster, often come with unpredictable weight variances that can throw off the magical science taking place in your oven. I always make a double batch of these biscuits, as they freeze quite well and thaw quickly.

Sablè di parmigiano al pimentón e mandarino
Tangerine and smoked paprika parmigiano biscuits

FOR 30 BISCUITS

4 ounces / 115 g grated parmigiano reggiano

4 ounces / 115 g unsalted butter, diced and chilled

4 ounces / 115 g all-purpose flour, plus more for dusting

1 teaspoon pimentón

1 teaspoon grated mandarin zest (or orange)

Lay a sheet of plastic wrap on a work surface. Combine all the ingredients in a food processor and pulse until you have pea-size pebbles. Turn the mixture out onto the plastic wrap and, preferably with cold hands, quickly press together into a puck. Enclose the puck in the plastic wrap and push out the air by rotating it between your hands while running your thumbs from top to bottom along the edges.

Seal the dough tightly in the plastic wrap and let rest in the refrigerator for at least half an hour or up to 2 days.

Line a sheet pan with parchment paper and heat the oven to 300°F / 150°C / gas mark 2.

To form the biscuits, divide the dough into 6 equal pieces and roll them into logs 1 inch / 2.5 cm in diameter. Flour your hands and slightly flatten the logs. Cut the dough on a slant into diamonds with a bench scraper.

Lay the diamonds on the prepared sheet pan, leaving ½ inch / 12 mm between one biscuit and the next. Place the sheet pan in the freezer for 10 to 15 minutes to harden the shaped biscuits.

Bake for 10 to 15 minutes, until the biscuits are a lovely golden blond and slightly crumbly around the bottom edge. Be mindful of the cooking time, as burnt parmigiano becomes quite bitter.

These biscuits are decadently crumbly when still warm, but try not to eat them all. Let them cool for all to enjoy. Store in an airtight container at room temperature for up to 1 week or freeze for up to 3 months.

This grown-up version of *pasta in bianco* (pasta with butter and cheese) is irresistible. It will both please an easy crowd and wipe the smirk off the face of the most exacting dinner guest. Snail-shaped shells hark back to the Italian childhood staple that is *pasta in bianco*, but any cut of pasta will do. Nutmeg or allspice—or even a zing of cayenne for heat—can take the place of the cinnamon.

Chiocciole al burro e parmigiano aromatiche
Spice-scented butter and parmigiano snail-shell pasta

Fill a pot with 3 quarts / 3 L water, cover it, and set it over heat to come to a boil. Season the boiling water with 1 tablespoon salt, drop in the pasta, stir, and cover the pot. Set a timer for 3 minutes shy of the suggested cooking time. When the water starts to boil again, remove the cover and adjust the heat so the water is at a lively, but not rolling, boil.

While the pasta is cooking, strip the marjoram leaves off the stems, save a few pretty leaves for garnishing, and finely chop the rest. Grate 2 teaspoons zest from the lemon. Halve the lemon and cut a thin slice for garnishing.

Melt the butter in a large frying pan over medium heat until it foams in the middle and is slightly yellow around the edges. Add the chopped marjoram, lemon zest, and cinnamon to the hot butter to cull their essence.

When the timer goes off, lift the shells out of the water with a handheld strainer and add to the frying pan. Raise the heat to high and add 1 cup / 240 ml of the pasta cooking water to finish cooking the pasta. Swirl and jostle the pan for 2 to 3 minutes to evenly distribute the flavors.

Dust the shells with the parmigiano and wet with 2 to 3 more spoonfuls of the pasta water, then stir vigorously to emulsify the dressing. Transfer the pasta to a warm serving platter. Sprinkle with a few drops of lemon juice, garnish with the saved marjoram and the lemon slice, and serve right away with more parmigiano on the side.

FOR 5 TO 6 PEOPLE

Salt and white pepper

1 package (1 pound / 450 g) chiocciole

2 marjoram sprigs

1 lemon

4 tablespoons / 60 g unsalted butter

½ teaspoon ground cinnamon

¼ cup / 60 ml grated parmigiano reggiano, plus more for serving

Popular beliefs are often kept alive by louder voices who hold steadfast to their convictions and aren't curious enough to look further. The no-cheese-with-fish rule is a blatant example of that. Seafood and dairy are not only common practices for young chefs all over Italy, but they are also found in long-established regional cookery. I was introduced to the pairing in this pasta by my friend Francesca Curtotti, a most talented and yet reluctant cook who has long been one of my gateways to the ingredients of the south. Calamarata pasta owes its name to the resemblance to calamari rings. Its large circular shape offers an ideal nesting place for the mussels, but if you cannot find it, use another wide tubular pasta.

Calamarata al pecorino e cozze
Calamarata pasta with pecorino and mussels

FOR 5 TO 6 PEOPLE

2½ pounds / 1.1 kg mussels

1 garlic clove

Salt and pepper

1 cup / 20 g loosely packed basil leaves

1 cup / 150 g cherry tomatoes

2 tablespoons extra-virgin olive oil, plus more for finishing

1 package (1 pound / 450 g) calamarata

¾ cup / 120 ml grated pecorino romano

Scrub the mussels then rinse them. Tap the shell of any open mussel; if it closes, keep it; but if it stays open, discard it. Rip off any hanging beards by pulling them down from the pointy tip to the curved end of the shell.

Put the mussels into a large sauté pan and seal it with a tight-fitting lid. Set the pan over high heat. In about 5 minutes, the mussels will open and release their juices. Turn off the heat. Discard any mussels that have remained close. Keep four or five open mussels whole for garnishing, then pick the flesh out of the rest of the shells, letting any juices drip back into the pan.

Filter the juices through a tight-mesh sieve or a colander lined with a paper towel to remove any grit. Keep the mussels and liquid refrigerated separately until ready to use them. Wipe the sauté pan cleanish.

Fill a pot with 3 quarts / 3 L water, cover it, and set it over heat to come to a boil.

While the water is coming to a boil, smash and peel the garlic, sprinkle it with a little salt, then mince into a paste. Stack the basil leaves, roll them up tightly lengthwise, and slice them crosswise into thin ribbons. Cut the tomatoes in half.

continued

Pour the olive oil into the sauté pan and add the garlic-salt paste and half of the basil. Heat on low for 3 to 4 minutes, until the garlic shows a little sizzle around the base and then turns glassy and hazy and the combined fragrances waft to your nose. Stand by the stove and swirl the pan occasionally so as not to burn the garlic.

The water should be boiling by now. Season it with 1½ teaspoons salt—the mix of mussels and pecorino delivers enough flavor that the water can be salted a little below the standard 1½ teaspoons per quart / 1 L. Stir the pasta into the boiling water and cover the pot. Set a timer for 3 minutes shy of the suggested cooking time. When the water starts to boil again, remove the cover and adjust the heat so the water is at a lively, but not rolling, boil.

Turn the heat to medium under the sauté pan and add the tomatoes. Stir and swirl for 2 to 3 minutes, until they look glossy. Gently push on the tomatoes to help release some liquid without squashing them. Let them soften for another couple of minutes, then pour the mussel juices back into the pan. Sample the sauce and season with pepper to suit your taste. Turn off the heat.

When the timer goes off, fish the pasta out of the water with a handheld strainer and add it to the sauté pan. Add about ½ cup / 120 ml of the pasta cooking water and turn the heat all the way up. Jostle and swirl the pan while the pasta finishes cooking and absorbs the liquids.

When the pasta is about 1 minute from done, stir in the pecorino and a couple of spoonfuls of pasta water. Stir vigorously to emulsify the fat and starchy water into a creamy coat. Toss in the mussels and finish with a splash of olive oil.

Transfer to a warm serving platter, garnish with the remaining basil, and serve right away.

As simple and obvious as this preparation is, it always hits the mark. The effort in assembling it is as minimal as the joy in savoring it will be unbound. These small flans (about 2 ounces / 60 g each) are quite rich, so resist the temptation to make the serving bigger. I find the lemon zest cuts through the cheesiness enough, but for an additional note of contrast, you can lightly lace them with some *aceto balsamico tradizionale*. I use pistachios because I love the color contrast, but you can swap them out for almonds or walnuts.

Sformatini di parmigiano e pistacchi
Parmigiano and pistachio tiny flans

Heat the oven to 325°F / 165°C / gas mark 3. Brush the cups of a 6-cup standard muffin pan with the butter. Fill a baking pan large enough to accommodate the muffin pan half full with hot water.

Roughly chop half of the pistachios and leave the rest whole.

Combine the cream, eggs, parmigiano, lemon zest, and salt in a measuring pitcher and mix with a handheld blender or a whisk until homogenous in color, emulsified, and somewhat airy. Season with pepper and grate in nutmeg until you can smell it without bending over the pitcher. Stir in the chopped pistachios.

Pour the batter into the muffin cups to within about ¼ inch / 6 mm of the rim. Place the water-filled baking pan as close to the oven as possible and open the oven door. Slide the muffin pan into the baking pan. Then carry the pans to the oven, trying your best to minimize the sloshing of the water.

Bake for 25 to 30 minutes, until the flans are puffy, slightly bouncy, and still soft to the touch. Remove from the oven and let cool in the water for 20 minutes. Take the muffin pan out of the baking pan and dry well.

To unmold the flans, run a small knife around the edge of each cup and tap the pan on the counter a few times to loosen the flans. Line a sheet pan with parchment paper and invert it over the muffin pan. Holding the two pans tightly together, invert them with one swift movement. Tap the bottom of each muffin cup, then gently shake the two-pan setup. Give the flans a minute or so to drop onto the parchment, then gently lift off the muffin pan.

Lift the tiny flans with an offset spatula, arrange them on small plates, and garnish them with the whole pistachios. Et voilà, a most flavorful and simple starter is ready. Serve warm.

FOR 6 FLANS

1 tablespoon unsalted butter, softened into a pomade

2 tablespoons raw pistachios

1 cup / 240 ml heavy cream

2 eggs

2½ ounces / 75 g grated parmigiano reggiano

2 teaspoons grated lemon zest

¼ teaspoon salt

White or black pepper

Nutmeg, for grating

For these tiny green flans, I have cut a new cloth from a flavor combination that is typically Sicilian. Feel free to give it your own regional or personal brushstroke. The escarole can be swapped out for anything green and leafy, from spinach to collard greens. The nuts and raisins are not a must, and you can use parmigiano in lieu of pecorino. Just follow the proportions and method and give yourself permission to play with your food.

Sformatini di scarola e pinoli al pecorino romano
Escarole and pine nuts tiny flans with pecorino romano

FOR 6 FLANS

1 tablespoon small raisins or dried currants

1 tablespoon unsalted butter, softened into a pomade

1 head escarole

2 eggs

1 cup / 240 ml heavy cream

2 tablespoons grated pecorino romano

2 teaspoons grated lemon zest

¼ teaspoon salt

½ to 1 teaspoon cayenne pepper

1 tablespoon pine nuts

Soak the raisins in warm water while you ready the other ingredients.

Heat the oven to 325°F / 165°C / gas mark 3. Brush the cups of a 6-cup standard muffin pan with the butter. Fill a baking pan large enough to accommodate the muffin pan half full with hot water.

Wash the escarole well and select 6 blemish-free large leaves. Steam the large leaves for 2 to 3 minutes, until just pliable enough to line the muffin cups. Cool the steamed leaves under cold water, pat dry, and use a leaf to upholster each buttered muffin cup, leaving a lot of overhang.

Bring a saucepan two-thirds full of water to a boil and drop the remaining escarole leaves into it. Cook for 5 to 6 minutes, until they are soft but still bright in color. Drain the escarole and let it cool until you can comfortably handle it, then wring the leaves until no more moisture can be extracted. Puree the greens in a food processor along with the eggs until smooth.

Transfer the batter to a measuring pitcher and add the cream, pecorino, lemon zest, and salt. Season with enough cayenne to satisfy your taste for heat. Beat with a handheld blender until the mixture is homogenous in color, well emulsified, and somewhat airy. Drain and squeeze the raisins. Stir them and the pine nuts into the batter.

Pour the mixture into the escarole-lined muffin cups, filling them to within about ¼ inch / 6 mm of the rim. Fold the overhang of the escarole leaves over to enclose the flans in an herby package. Place the water-filled baking pan as close to the oven as possible and open the oven door. Slide the muffin pan into the baking pan, being careful not to let water splash into the batter. Then slowly carry the pans to the oven, trying your best to minimize the sloshing of the water.

Bake for 25 to 30 minutes, until the escarole leaves feel a little tighter and the flans are slightly bouncy and still soft to the touch. Remove from the oven and let cool in the water for 20 minutes. Take the muffin pan out of the baking pan and dry well.

To unmold the flans, run a small knife around the edge of each cup and tap the muffin pan on the counter a few times to loosen the flans. Line a sheet pan with parchment paper and invert it over the muffin pan. Holding the two pans tightly together, invert them with one swift movement. Tap the bottom of each muffin cup with a knife handle or a spoon, then gently shake the two-pan setup. Give the flans a minute or so to drop onto the parchment, then gently lift off the muffin pan.

Lift a tiny flan with an offset spatula and arrange it on a small plate. Do the same with the other 5 flans and serve while still warm.

Mushrooms prepared this way have become a recurring Thanksgiving side in my home, but the dish is also hearty enough to serve as a main course. I always make more than I expect to need, as the leftovers make a delightful pasta sauce. I favor thyme as a complement to mushrooms, but rosemary, sage, or savory will also work well.

Funghi di bosco al cartoccio con pecorino e timo
Wild mushrooms en papillote with pecorino and thyme

Heat the oven to 350°F / 180°C / gas mark 4.

Free the mushrooms of dirt and other debris with a brush and trim the stem ends. Chunk the bigger ones irregularly and leave the smaller ones whole. Place in a bowl.

Slice the shallot paper-thin. Toss them into the mushroom bowl.

Add the thyme sprigs to the mushrooms. Season with 1 teaspoon salt and pepper to suit your taste. Toss well. Shower with the olive oil and toss again.

Lay a piece of aluminum foil large enough to contain the mushrooms with lots of space left over on a sheet pan. Line the foil with parchment paper and place the seasoned mushrooms in the center. Dust the mushrooms with the pecorino.

Marry the long sides of the foil and parchment and fold them together to seal closed. Then crunch the ends of your packet shut.

Slide the pan into the oven and bake the mushrooms for 45 minutes. Bring the packet to the table and slit it open with scissors while watching your guests rejoice in an unforgettable olfactory experience before eating the mushrooms.

FOR 6 PEOPLE

2 pounds / 1 kg mixed wild mushrooms

1 shallot

4 thyme sprigs

Salt and pepper

¼ cup / 60 ml extra-virgin olive oil

¼ cup / 60 ml grated pecorino romano

CHAPTER 8

MOZZARELLA, RICOTTA, & BURRATA

Intensely delicate flavors with short lives

Of all the things life in Italy has got going for it, the fact that mozzarella and ricotta are part of any weight-loss regime definitely makes the top five.

In Italy we so love our mozzarella, we have given it the TSG—traditional gastronomic specialty—insignia. In other words: the rest of the world can keep making it, but it's never going to be as good.

Mozzarella starts as whole milk, which undergoes a very light acidic fermentation before welcoming rennet to create curd. The curd is diced into hazelnut-size pieces and left to coagulate. The coagulate is laid on a counter to lose moisture, then cut again and melted in hot water, then kneaded and spun until it gathers into a glossy, homogeneous amalgam. The amalgam is sheared into strips. The strips go into a fresh vat of hot water for the last round of stretching and pulling before being cinched and lopped off into a ball.

What separates acceptable from addictive mozzarella are good ingredients and skilled humans along the line of production. Milk for artisanal mozzarella is always fresh, fermentation happens with carefully tended starter cultures grown from the cheese dairy's own whey, and the final pulling and lopping stages are done by hand to impart the right amount of tension to leave the eyes from which milky tears spring when the cheese is sliced. Industrially produced mozzarella uses frozen milk fermented with synthetic cultures and relies on citric acid to add the tangy note. Commercial mozzarella balls have an even texture that is either too dense or too mushy.

Cheese-pulling techniques have been around for millennia in the Mediterranean basin. The mention of cheese called mozza—"cut off"—first appears in Italian food history in the twelfth century. By the sixteenth century, the name has taken the distinctly southern Italian diminutive of mozzarella. It is still a limited-edition fresh craft for the wealthy landowners of the Italian south. In the early twentieth century, with the advent of refrigeration and train transport, mozzarella finally finds its way to the rest of the country.

The best mozzarella is still the prerogative of the south's centuries of artisanal wisdom. Puglia, in the southeast, is the cradle of cow's milk mozzarella—fiordilatte—while the southwestern region of Campania is world famous for its buffalo milk mozzarella, or bufala. Fiordilatte is creamy white and glossy. It tastes sweeter and comes undone in the mouth in a continuous, moist, cloud-like feel. Bufala is matte porcelain white. Its taste is distinctively but pleasantly sour. The skin slightly resists at first bite to give way to milky spurts.

It goes without saying that both territories lay claim to the superiority of their own and that their people endlessly debate about which one came first. It doesn't matter; they're both so stellar that each has gained a PDO seal. Puglia's mozzarella di Gioia del Colle and mozzarella di bufala campana are considered the best in the country and critical to the agricultural and human ecosystem of their areas of production. As always, look for the red-and-gold seal when buying either.

I had this boyfriend once, back in New York, who couldn't understand what made ricotta something without which I couldn't live, and then I took him to Italy. He ate ricotta warm, sliced into soft, creamy slabs rather than blobbed refrigerator-cold on a plate. He soon fell into the Italian habit of eating ricotta with a sprinkle of sugar and cocoa or coffee powder, or with olive oil and salt. His newfound respect for ricotta long outlasted our relationship.

Italian ricotta is in a league of its own. Cato the Elder, in 200 BCE, describes the making of ricotta as a nourishing afterthought of cheese making. Its name is a literal iteration of *cotta*—"cooked"—meaning it is cooked twice. Indeed, ricotta is not technically a cheese; it is a by-product of the very first whey left after cheese making, which the Italian Ministry of Agriculture defines as a product of animal origin.

To make ricotta, the whey is reheated and lightly stirred so the coagulate still floating around gathers into flakes. The flakes are fished out with a tightly meshed strainer and dropped into baskets. The baskets are left to drain until their contents settles into the tremulous wonder that is ricotta. Fresh ricotta is best in its first three days of life. It will last a week, but starting from day four, the balance of sweet and sour starts tipping toward the latter. The yellowing of ricotta betrays that the sour is veering to acid. Before discarding it, peel the layers and you might find that the heart is still milky and sweet.

Ricotta can come from the whey of any type of milk. Cow and sheep are the most common in Italy, and one can even buy *ricotta di latte misto*, made from a mix of the two. But its cheese-adjacent nature means that quality ricotta needs quality cheese production. It is not by chance, then, that the most prized ricottas hail from the same places as some of Italy's most prized cheeses.

Ricotta romana PDO is the little sister of pecorino romano. She is packed in the characteristic truncated cone shape and can weigh up to four pounds (two kilograms). It is made exclusively with sheep's milk whey and a little salt and is at once grainy and creamy, lemony and sugary. It stands on its own and also makes a wonderful background for other dishes. It isn't easy to find outside of Italy, but if you see the yellow-and-red square with a sheep's snout in between two uppercase Rs, snatch it right away, run home, and eat it before everyone else knows you have it.

In southern areas of buffalo mozzarella production, the whey is used for ricotta so good it has also gotten the PDO seal of quality. Buffalo ricotta can have buffalo cream added to make it more compact and/or starter culture to calibrate acidity. It is granular without being sandy, creamy but not buttery, light and dense all at once. The authenticity of the product is marked by the words ricotta di bufala campana in red and green circling the head of a buffalo stylized in black.

In the last twenty to twenty-five years, delicate thermal pasteurization and airtight packaging in whey have lengthened the life of ricotta and made its export possible, if not frequent. If you have to rely on domestically produced fresh ricotta, use whole-milk ones made by small local dairies. Partially skimmed large-production ricotta is packed with stabilizers that can throw off recipes.

Ricotta also comes in *salata*—"salted"—form. Ricotta salata is ricotta left to compact by extracting moisture with a salt bath. The moisture leaches out while the salt slithers in, resulting in a compact, friable cheese whose purpose is to be grated or shaved to finish dishes.

Burrata is the sexiest cheese that ever lived. Glossy, soft, and caressable, it declares its peak by seeping curves of cream with a delicately exciting flavor. This goddess of the cheese world found its cult status in a relatively short time.

Burrata sees the light in the 1920s when the owners of a dairy in the town of Andria in Puglia made virtue out of necessity. When a snowstorm blocks transport routes, the Bianchino brothers transform as much milk as they can into mozzarella. As the rest of the milk starts separating, they use the cream top to drown the leftovers of mozzarella making. Realizing that the ethereal mixture wouldn't last long, they wrap it with mozzarella skin and then seal it by choking it at the neck with a string. A century later, burrata made in Andria is still considered the best one, and its production is safeguarded by an PGI seal.

It has taken a while for burrata to take the world by storm, as its short shelf life kept it close to its area of origin for some time. Even as I was growing up in the 1970s, burrata was that rare and precious gift someone traveling to Puglia would bring back. The evolution of transport and packaging has turned the tide on burrata's fortunes. Today's burrata is packed in hermetically sealed containers that prolong its shelf life enough to export it all over the globe.

To experience burrata at its best, leave it at room temperature for twenty to thirty minutes before serving it. The filling will soften and cream will run out as the skin is opened. In the kitchen, burrata is never cooked but rather paired. Add it to hot pasta or strew it over pizza just out of the oven. It goes well with many fruits and vegetables and matches quite heavenly with tomatoes. Try it with caviar, *bottarga*, or with a delicate fish crudo, and you'll discover that the old adage about fish and cheese isn't quite accurate.

Before we head to the stove, I urge you to savor these three ingredients first in their natural state, then topped with a little olive oil and a few flakes of salt, and finally drizzled with a little honey. Only then can you fully understand their nature and the infinite possibilities they offer.

Nothing screams spring as loudly as peas and green garlic, but if you love these crostini so much that you find yourself craving them all the time, you can use frozen new peas and regular garlic. I always make a little more of the spread than I need as it can double as a quick sauce for pasta. Dilute it with some pasta water and scatter with toasted nuts for crunch, then toss any cut of pasta with it.

Crostini di piselli novelli, aglietto e ricotta di bufala
Shelling peas, green garlic, and buffalo ricotta crostini

Fill a saucepan with 1 quart / 1 L water and set it over heat to come to a boil.

Clean the green garlic much like you would a scallion: trim off the bottom hairy root and the top third of the green leaves and remove the outer layer. Set aside a 1-inch / 2.5-cm piece of the white part of 1 stalk, then cut all the rest into chunks. If you are using garlic cloves, smash and peel them. Cut one-third off 1 garlic clove and set it aside for finishing. Pluck the mint leaves from the stems and save the 12 prettiest leaves as a garnish.

Season the boiling water with 1 teaspoon salt. Drop the peas, green garlic chunks or 1⅔ garlic cloves, and the mint leaves into the pot. Cook for 10 to 12 minutes, until the garlic is soft and the peas are tender and still bright green.

While the vegetables are cooking, mince the saved green garlic or garlic cloves and zest half of the lemon. Mix them together.

Save 2 tablespoons of the cooking water, then drain the vegetables. Rinse them with cold water to keep the bright color, then transfer them to a food processor. Puree into a textured and easily spreadable cream, adding a splash of the cooking water if the mixture seems too thick to spread. Sample a spoonful and season with salt and pepper to best suit your palate.

Cut the baguette on a slant into 12 slices each ⅛ inch / 3 mm thick and toast them until they have a blush of gold, some outer resistance, and a soft heart.

Brush the warm baguette slices with olive oil and spread them with a layer of ricotta followed by a layer of green spread. Finish the crostini with a thread of olive oil, a touch of the garlic–lemon zest mince, and a scant dusting of pepper. Garnish with a leaf of mint. Serve them soon, as the bread can get soggy from the ricotta.

FOR 12 CROSTINI

2 green garlic stalks (or 2 garlic cloves)

1 to 2 mint sprigs

Salt and pepper

1 cup / 140 g shelled English peas

1 lemon

Extra-virgin olive oil as needed

10 ounces / 280 g buffalo ricotta (if unavailable, substitute cow's or sheep's milk ricotta)

½ baguette

Mozzarella is a lady and the bread is her chariot in this classic of Roman cuisine. Typically, this sandwich is a repurposing of staples that are past their prime. It uses day-old bread and mozzarella that has lost its milky moisture. The classic version calls for an anchovy, but you can make it vegetarian by omitting it or notch it up for the omnivores with some prosciutto or mortadella.

Mozzarella in carrozza
Crispy mozzarella sandwich

FOR 4 SANDWICHES

8 slices bread, each ¼ inch / 6 mm thick

Salt and pepper

1 ball (8 ounces / 225 g) fresh mozzarella (or two 4-ounce / 115-g balls)

8 anchovy fillets packed in oil

1 cup / 240 ml whole milk

½ cup / 70 g all-purpose flour

2 eggs

1½ cups / 170 g unseasoned dried breadcrumbs

Vegetable oil, for deep-frying

If the bread you are using has a very hard crust, slice it off; otherwise, you can leave it on. Either way, line up the bread slices in two rows of 4 slices on a cutting board and sprinkle them with salt.

Cut the mozzarella into 8 slices, pat them dry, and arrange 2 slices over each piece of bread in the bottom row, leaving a ¼-inch / 6-mm empty margin all around the edges. Lay 2 anchovy fillets on top of each mozzarella-topped bread slice. Dust with some pepper and cover with the undressed bread slices. Press each sandwich down and secure it with two toothpicks.

Pour the milk into a medium bowl and put the flour on a plate. Beat the eggs in a second medium bowl. Spread the breadcrumbs on a small sheet pan.

Dip 2 sandwiches into the milk until soaked through but not dripping. Dredge them in the flour, then shake them until the flour forms a thin veil around the bread. Immerse the sandwiches in the eggs until they are completely coated and drippy, then place them on the breadcrumbs. Dredge all sides of the sandwiches in the crumbs multiple times, until they are fully and evenly coated in a thick layer of crumbs. Pat the coating so it adheres well to the sandwiches. Repeat with the other 2 sandwiches.

Choose a shallow saucepan or deep sauté pan wide enough for all 4 sandwiches to comfortably swim in it at once. Pour the oil to a depth of 2 inches / 5 cm into the pan and heat to 340°F / 170°C on a thermometer. If you do not have a thermometer, you can test the temperature by dropping a small cube of bread into the oil. If the oil is hot enough, the bread will not sink and will emit a faint sizzle and release lots of lively bubbles.

Very carefully lower a sandwich into the hot oil; when it's about ½ inch / 12 mm in, let it slide in. Repeat with the other 3 sandwiches. For your safety, do not drop the sandwich straight into the pan or splashes of scalding oil will burn

you. If you do not have a pan wide enough to hold all the sandwiches, you can fry them in batches. Place a sheet pan lined with a cooling rack as close as possible to where you are deep-frying.

Fry the sandwiches, adjusting the heat up or down as needed to maintain the temperature within 10°F / 5°C of where it started. After 5 to 6 minutes, flip the sandwiches with tongs to cook evenly on both sides. After having been in the hot oil for a total 10 to 12 minutes, the sandwiches should be a deep golden all over. If necessary, cook a little longer, spooning hot oil on the top.

Lift the sandwiches out of the oil with a slotted spoon or a spider and move them to the cooling rack to let any excess oil drain. Sprinkle with salt and let cool for a few minutes before serving.

The sauce happened during one of the summers I spent teaching in Puglia when I forgot some cherry tomatoes in a low oven for half an hour longer than planned. The recipe requires very short active cooking time but unattended long cooking times, so I like to divide the work into chunks. Take fifteen minutes of tomato prepping time between coffee and breakfast and leave the tomatoes to drain even for the whole day. As soon as you get home from work, slide the tomatoes into the oven, get into soft clothes, and have a drink. When dinnertime nears, the sauce will be ready and boiling the pasta will be the only involved task left.

Orecchiette con pomodorini infornati e burrata
Orecchiette with roasted cherry tomatoes and burrata

Halve the tomatoes, transfer to a bowl, and season them with 2 teaspoons salt. Pluck a handful of leaves from the various stems and save them for finishing. Smash and peel the garlic cloves. Add the remaining herbs and the garlic to the tomatoes. Toss well, tip into a colander set over a bowl and let sit for 30 minutes to lose some moisture.

In preparation for your kitchen to smell divine, heat the oven to 325°F / 165°C / gas mark 3. Line a sheet pan with parchment.

Toss and shake the tomatoes then pour them onto the sheet pan in one layer. Bake for 45 minutes, until the skins are wrinkled and have a few burnt tips.

Fill a pot with 3 quarts / 3 L water, cover it, and set it over heat to come to a boil. Season it with 1 tablespoon salt, stir in the orecchiette, and cover the pot. When the water starts to boil again, remove the cover and adjust the heat so the water is at a lively, but not rolling, boil. Continue cooking until the pasta is al dente—generally 1 minute shy of the suggested cooking time.

Pick the herbs sprigs and garlic out of the tomatoes and discard them. Pour the tomatoes into a warm serving bowl. Sample and adjust salt and pepper to your taste. Douse with the oil and mix well.

Fish the ready pasta out of the water with a handheld strainer, add it to the roasted tomatoes, and toss well. If the tomatoes are clumping, add 1 or 2 spoonfuls of pasta cooking water.

Scatter the saved herbs on top. Tear open the burrata and stream it across the orecchiette. Drizzle with a thread of olive oil and serve right away. Each diner should get some burrata to mix into the hot pasta.

FOR 4 TO 6 PEOPLE

2 pounds / 900 g cherry tomatoes

Salt and pepper

10 to 12 mixed herb sprigs (thyme, oregano, marjoram, basil, and mint all work)

2 garlic cloves

1 package (1 pound / 450 g) orecchiette

¼ cup / 60 ml extra-virgin olive oil, plus more for finishing

5 to 8 ounces / 140 to 225 g burrata

Of the rather tumultuous last-minute lunch at Giuseppe and Francesca's home, I remember the unease when they turned to me. I had been in their wedding party as one of the witnesses whose signature Italian law requires for a wedding to be legal, and they both expected support for their side of their heated argument. Mediating became easier when the pasta was served. Ten years later, their marriage is stronger than ever, and the pasta is still with me.

Passito—literally "withered"—is sweet wine from grapes that are left to ripen past their prime, either on the vine or after they've been harvested. Once the grapes have reached the appropriate sugar concentration, they are pressed into wine. Several ones fall under this category; this recipe was made with the Sicilian Malvasia delle Lipari. If you can't find Sicilian *passito*, use another sweet wine, like Vin Santo, Sauternes, or, in a pinch, even a dry vermouth.

Pennette alle cipolle rosse, salvia e vino passito siciliano con ricotta salata

Penne with red onion, sage, and sweet wine with ricotta salata

FOR 5 TO 6 PEOPLE

2 medium red onions

5 to 6 sage leaves

4 ounces / 115 g ricotta salata

3 tablespoons extra-virgin olive oil

Salt and pepper

1 cup / 240 ml passito

1 package (1 pound / 450 g) pennette

Cut the onions in half from stem to root end. Place an onion half cut side down on a cutting board with the stem to root line perpendicular to you. With a sharp knife, go all across the onion dome from right to left—or left to right if you are left-handed—cutting the onion into scythes ¼ inch / 6 mm thick. Repeat with the remaining onion halves. This technique ensures that the onions will retain some texture in the center when cooked.

Leave 1 or 2 of the prettier, smaller sage leaves whole for garnish. Stack the rest, roll them up tightly lengthwise, and cut them crosswise into thin ribbons. Shave the ricotta salata.

Fill a pot with 3 quarts / 3 L water, cover it and set it over heat to come to a boil.

While the water is coming to a boil, pour 2 tablespoons of the olive oil into a large sauté pan, add the sliced sage, and place over medium heat until the combined fragrances of the oil and sage waft to your nostrils. Add the onions and 1 teaspoon salt. Raise the heat to medium-high and cook, swirling the pan often, for 2 to 3 minutes, just until the onions are beginning to sweat and wilt.

Douse with the wine. When the wine has evaporated enough that it no longer smells acidic, lower the heat to medium, cover partially, and continue

braising for 4 to 6 minutes, until the onions have a pink haze on the concave side and are just tender but still retain their shape. Sample an onion scythe and adjust salt and pepper to suit your palate.

The water should be boiling by now. Season it with 2 teaspoons salt, stir in the pennette, and cover the pot. Set a timer for 2 minutes shy of the suggested cooking time. When the water starts to boil again, remove the cover and adjust the heat so the water is at a lively, but not rolling, boil.

When the timer goes off, fish the pasta out of the water with a handheld strainer and add it to the sauté pan with the onions and sage. Raise the heat to high and add ½ cup / 120 ml of the pasta cooking water. Swirl and jostle the pan for a couple of minutes to finish cooking the pasta, adding a touch more cooking water if necessary. Turn off the heat.

Save a few shavings of ricotta for garnishing and throw the rest into the pan. Finish with the last tablespoon of olive oil and toss well to meld all the flavor elements.

Tip the pasta onto a warm serving platter, top with the saved ricotta shavings and the whole sage leaves, and serve right away.

I love premade doughs for tarts and pies. There, I said it—what a weight off my chest. They are a shortcut no one ever detects, and they are infinitely versatile. For this tart, I like to use puff pastry because the simplicity of the topping benefits from the additional layers of texture and flavor. You can cheat even further by using red peppers roasted, packed in water in a jar, and placed on a market shelf by someone else, though your more exacting diners might catch you.

Sfogliata di mozzarella e peperoni
Peppers and mozzarella flaky tart

If the puff pastry is frozen, thaw according to the package directions.

Heat the oven to 350°F / 190°C / gas mark 4. Line a sheet pan with parchment paper and place the bell peppers on it. Slide into the oven. Roast for about 25 minutes, until the skin has burnt spots and the peppers have collapsed and wrinkled. Grab them with tongs, drop them into a brown paper bag, roll the top of the bag closed, and let sit for 10 minutes. This technique makes the peppers easy to peel. Leave the oven on.

Meanwhile, line a plate with a paper towel. Drain the mozzarella and chop it roughly, then place it on the paper towel to lose moisture. If using fresh oregano, strip the leaves off the sprig and finely chop them. Break the egg into a small bowl and lightly whisk it. Peel the peppers, cut them in half, and remove the core, filaments, and seeds. Pat them dry and slice into strips ¼ inch / 6 mm wide along the ribbing.

Line the sheet pan with fresh parchment paper. Lay the puff pastry sheet on the parchment and prick it in 8 to 10 spots with a fork. Sprinkle the pastry with a pinch of salt and scatter the mozzarella over it, leaving a 1½-inch / 4-cm clear border around the edges. Dust the mozzarella with the parmigiano and oregano, then season it with 1 teaspoon salt and the pepper.

Arrange the roasted pepper strips over the tart in whatever pattern you fancy, staying clear of the empty edges. On the day Molly and I shot the tart's portrait, my fancy was an attempt at a corn stalk. Loosely roll the uncovered pastry edge onto itself until it borders the peppers.

Slide the tart into the oven and set a timer for 30 minutes. When the timer goes off, brush the edges of the tart with the beaten egg and slide it back into the oven. Set the timer for another 15 minutes. When the timer goes off, your tart is done. Let it rest and cool a little before eating.

FOR 8 TO10 PEOPLE

1 pound / 450 g puff pastry

2 red bell peppers

1 orange or yellow bell pepper

1 ball (8 ounces / 225 g) fresh mozzarella

1 oregano sprig, or 1 teaspoon dried oregano

1 egg

Salt

2 tablespoons grated parmigiano reggiano

Pinch of pepper

I cannot find a base this dessert does not hit: it is fast and simple to assemble, improves after sitting for a few hours, is gluten-free, and can be made any time of year by using seasonal fruit. And it is both original and delectable to boot.

Trifle di ricotta montata al miele con amaretti, pesche e vino dolce
Whipped honeyed ricotta trifle with amaretti, peaches, and dessert wine

FOR 4 PEOPLE

1 ripe but firm large peach

1 cup / 240 ml dessert wine of your choice

12 ounces / 340 g ricotta

1½ tablespoons honey

12 amaretti

Chill four ½-cup / 120-ml glasses in the refrigerator.

Halve and pit the peach and cut each half into 8 crescents. Place them in a bowl and douse with the wine. Toss well and leave the peach slices to marinate while you prepare the rest of the ingredients.

Combine the ricotta and honey in a bowl and whisk them with glee until the ricotta appears smooth and glossy. Crumble the amaretti.

Retrieve the glasses from the refrigerator and plop a generous spoonful of ricotta in the bottom of each glass. Shake the glasses to spread the cheese, arrange 2 peach slices on the ricotta, and sprinkle with amaretti crumbles. Repeat the layers. Drizzle each glass with a bit of the peach marinade.

Seal the glasses with plastic wrap and refrigerate for at least 1 hour or up to 1 day before serving.

If you are short on time, long on imagination, and looking to impress with your cooking, *crostata* is the dessert for you. Think of it as the pasta of desserts, a blank canvas you can brush in any stroke. *Pasta frolla*, the dough used for *crostata*, is a shortcrust that can enshrine any kind of combination of fruit, jam, cheese, chocolate, and nuts. A *crostata* can be open-faced or a double crust, with a lattice or crimped, fluted or straight, round or with angles.

Among many options, ricotta is one of my favorites for filling a *crostata*. The adaptably unique character of this cheese makes it well suited for a tart in guises that go from the elementary to the elaborate.

I have divided this recipe into two sections. The first is a detailed account of how to make a really good *pasta frolla*. The second section will give you the basic proportion for a ricotta filling followed by four different ideas to give your ricotta tart a distinct personality.

Crostate di ricotta
Ricotta tarts

Pasta frolla / Italian sugar crust

There are many versions of pasta frolla. Mine is adapted from Science in the Kitchen and the Art of Eating Well by Pellegrino Artusi, first published in 1891. I swear by it as do the many home cooks to whom I've taught it over the last decade. But in the unlikelihood a reader does not like it, I encourage that reader to find a version more suited to their taste.

The original version of this crust has a percentage of lard, which pushes friability to the next level. If you have a good source and the right crowd, try swapping out one-third of the butter for lard. Baker's sugar—also known as caster, superfine, or ultra-fine—makes the dough easier to roll out, but granulated sugar will also do.

Pasta frolla freezes well, so I always make more than I need. Thaw it on the counter for about an hour before getting it mold-ready with a rolling pin.

Removable bottom pans and tart rings make crostata handling easy. Or use a shallow sheet or pie pan and serve the tart straight from the pan. Always line the pan with parchment paper, even if nonstick, so the crostata will release without a fuss.

continued

MAKES ENOUGH DOUGH FOR TWO 10-INCH / 25-CM OPEN-FACED TARTS, ONE 10-INCH / 25-CM DOUBLE-CRUST TART, ONE 10-INCH / 25-CM TART WITH LATTICE TOP WITH LEFTOVER DOUGH FOR COOKIES, OR SIX 3-INCH / 7.5-CM INDIVIDUAL TARTS

9½ ounces / 270 g all-purpose flour

3½ ounces / 100 g baker's or granulated sugar

Pinch of salt

Grated zest of 1 lemon or ½ orange

4¾ ounces / 135 g unsalted butter, diced and chilled

4 yolks from large eggs

To make it accessible to everyone, I have developed four different methods for mixing this crust. If you have a well-equipped kitchen, a stand mixer is the fastest way, but it can also be made in a food processor—a more common appliance—using a handheld pastry cutter, or even, last but not least, entirely by hand.

Stand mixer method: Combine the flour, sugar, salt, and zest in the mixer bowl. Fit the mixer with the paddle attachment, place the shield on the bowl, and stir on speed 2. Add the butter and yolks and increase the speed to 4.

As the butter and yolks are broken up into the dry ingredients, the mixture will turn into thick, uneven, powdery chunks. Raise the speed to 6.

The chunks will quickly turn to crumbs of more even size and still be whitish and powdery. Accelerate to speed 8.

In a matter of seconds, the small crumbs will lose their powderiness and become yellow. You can now move the speed all the way up to 10.

Tune your ears to the noise of the paddle. The shift will be subtle, but as the crumbs cluster into clumps, the rotating arm will sound as if it's catching, as if the dough is resisting the paddling. As soon as you hear that change, turn off the mixer. The crumbs will be yellow with the occasional fleck of butter and will have clustered in larger pieces. The whole process should take 3 minutes at the most. Each step at a different speed is a matter of seconds.

Lay two squares of plastic wrap on the counter and pour half of the clumped dough onto each one. Working with one at a time, gather the dough in the center and bring together the four corners of the plastic wrap. Twist them together to press the clumps into a mass. Flatten and shape the mass into a thick puck and wrap tightly. Holding the package in your hands from its sides, turn it while pressing together with your palms and sliding your thumbs from top to bottom all around to push out excess air. Repeat with the second half of the dough.

Tighten the plastic wrap and let the dough rest in the refrigerator for at least 30 minutes to set and harden before rolling it out. If you do not use the pasta frolla within a week, freeze it.

Food processor method: Place all the ingredients in a food processor and pulse until reduced to yellow large clumps with a few visible flecks of butter. This could take up to a minute. Proceed as directed in the mixer method.

Pastry cutter method: Stir together the flour, sugar, salt, and zest in a bowl. Add the butter and yolks and work them with a pastry cutter, occasionally tossing and jostling the bowl. Continue until the mixture is reduced to yellow large clumps with a few visible flecks of butter. Proceed as directed in the mixer method.

Hand method: If you own none of the above trappings, you can make pasta frolla entirely by hand. Stir together the flour, sugar, salt, and zest in a bowl. Add the butter and yolks. Mix with a wooden spoon to break the yolks. Crumble the butter by swishing your fingertips against the heel of your hands, as if playing castanets. Jostle the bowl to toss its contents, then swirl them, using your fingers as if they were salad servers. Alternate swishing, tossing, and swirling until the ingredients are reduced to yellow large clumps with a few visible flecks of butter. Proceed as directed in the mixer method.

When ready to roll out the dough, lightly flour your work surface and a rolling pin. The ideal surface for rolling is marble because of the low temperature it maintains, followed by stainless steel and then wood. If using wood, ensure that the board is free of any strong odors from previous uses. Ideally, you have a wooden board that is dedicated to sweets.

Spread the flour in an evenly thin veil. Unwrap the rested dough, set it on the floured surface, and soften it by administering a few decisive whacks with the rolling pin. It will make for more expedient rolling.

Roll the dough from the center toward the outer edges, following the shape of your chosen mold. Visualize the task as a compass and its four cardinal points: roll once from the center to the north, then from the center to the east, south, and west. Smooth the compass three or four times, then slightly lift it, turn it 90 degrees, and repeat. Rolling and turning in all four directions will translate even pressure into even thickness. Lifting will prevent sticking to the surface. If globs of excess flour sneak their way into your dough, brush them away.

When you get to ⅛ inch / 3 mm thickness, roll the dough around your rolling pin, lift, and carefully unroll it on the mold, letting it drape toward the center. Press in the dough to line the mold completely, then lightly press the rolling pin around the edge to excise the excess crust. Should the dough break, just align the dough scraps and pinch them together. The shell will keep its size and shape.

Prick the bottom of the shell with a fork and refrigerate to set and harden while you prepare the filling. You can also freeze the ready-to-use crostata shell; just wrap it well to keep it from absorbing odors. When ready to use—it should be within 3 months—it will defrost in the time it takes you to fill it.

8 ounces / 225 g ricotta

¼ cup / 50 g baker's
or granulated sugar

2 eggs, at room
temperature

Ripieno di ricotta semplice per crostata / Basic ricotta tart filling

This easy-to-remember mixture is the paving for many a version of ricotta-filled tarts. Take it from here and ride it wherever your cooking imagination leads you.

Baker's sugar dissolves faster than granulated, though either will do. Sifting the ricotta is important to smooth its graininess. If you plan to make your tart right away, fluffing the egg whites to stiff peaks will result in an airier filling, If you are prepping it in advance, then do not bother with egg whipping; just mix in the whole eggs as they are and store the filling in the refrigerator for no longer than 3 days.

Place a tight-mesh strainer over a bowl and press the ricotta through it with a rubber spatula. Add the sugar and gleefully stir with a wooden spoon until the mixture appears smooth and is glossy but not shiny.

If you are using the filling right away, separate the eggs and work the yolks into the ricotta until they are homogeneously mixed. Whip the whites to stiff peaks by hand or with an electric mixer. Stir one-fourth of the whipped whites into the ricotta mixture to loosen it. Fold in the rest of the whites in two batches, using a rubber spatula in a circular bottom-to-top motion.

If you are making the filling in advance, stir the eggs into the ricotta and sugar mixture until they are well amalgamated and there are no streaks of a different color.

You can use this filling as is for a double-crust tart, but if I were you, I would use the following recipes to tart it up.

Al profumo di limone / Lemon scented

This simplest among ricotta tarts occupies a special place in my story of food. In the twilight hours of a spring day in 1999, a week away from the opening of my Madison Avenue store, I was in its kitchen working on giving this tart its own New York City personality, one that could not rely on the lemons from a garden in Sorrento my friend Rita Pane uses for the recipe in her brilliant book, *Sapori del Sud*. A tall, distinguished woman walked in. She had the kind and mysterious aura I imagined around my great-aunt Ginny, about whose beauty and irreverence my grandmother would grumble with displayed disapproval and hidden longing. The woman and I flowed into an easy conversation about tarts, inspirations, food, Italy, and what brought me where I was. Words hung for a moment when she introduced herself. She was Florence Fabricant, the weather vane that had guided my food choices for the last decade. Shortly after that memorable meeting, she would be the first to feature my short-lived shop, Buitoni & Garretti, in the New York Times.

Position a rack in the lower third of the oven and heat the oven to 375°F / 190°C / gas mark 5.

Stir the lemon zest and limoncello into the ricotta filling.

Pour the filling into the tart shell. It should come up almost to the rim. Tap the mold on the counter a few times to level the filling. Gently cover the tart with the pasta frolla round, paying mind not to make it too taut. Press all around the edges to seal. Cut off any excess crust.

Place the tart on a sheet pan and slide the pan onto the lower rack of the oven. Bake for 40 to 45 minutes, until the edges of the tart are beigy brown and the top has puffed up.

Let cool completely and dust lightly with confectioners' sugar before serving. I doubt the tart will last that long, but it will be delectable for at least 3 days if stored in a cool, dry place.

MAKES ONE 10-INCH / 25-CM TART; FOR 8 TO 10 PEOPLE

Grated zest of 3 lemons

1 tablespoon limoncello, or grated zest of 1 more lemon

2 cups / 400 g basic ricotta tart filling

One 10-inch / 25-cm pasta frolla tart shell

One 11-inch / 28-cm pasta frolla round rolled ⅛ inch / 3 mm thick

Confectioners' sugar, for dusting

MAKES ONE 10-INCH /
25-CM TART;
FOR 8 TO 10 PEOPLE

¼ cup / 40 g plus
2 tablespoons chipped
bittersweet chocolate

½ cups / 400 g basic
ricotta tart filling

One 10-inch / 25-cm
pasta frolla tart shell

One 11-inch / 28-cm pasta
frolla round rolled ⅛ inch /
3 mm thick

Al cioccolato amaro / With bittersweet chocolate

Chocolate and ricotta are a common combination in Italy. Indeed, one of my favorite snacks is a small bowl of ricotta dusted with bittersweet cocoa powder and sprinkled with sugar. Some version of this dessert is likely to be found at a kid's birthday party or nibbled with afternoon tea. I prefer to chip my own chocolate because I enjoy the uneven bursts of flavor strewing the ricotta, but chocolate chips will work too.

Position a rack in the lower third of the oven and heat the oven to 375°F / 190°C / gas mark 5.

Stir ¼ cup / 40 g of the chocolate into the ricotta filling.

Pour the filling into the tart shell. It should fill almost to the rim. Tap the mold on the counter a few times to level the filling.

Cut the dough round into strips ¼ inch / 6 mm wide. Arrange them in a lattice pattern on top of the ricotta, pressing the ends to the bottom crust to seal. Distribute the remaining 2 tablespoons chips of chocolate so they peek out from the small windows created by the lattice.

Place the tart on a sheet pan and slide the pan onto the lower rack of the oven. Bake for 40 to 45 minutes, until the edges of the tart are beigy brown and the top has puffed up slightly.

This tart is best fresh and warm. I let it cool just enough not to burn the roof of my mouth before serving it. If some is left over, keep it in a cool, dry place for a couple of days. The ricotta will sag into some density and make a fantastic breakfast dipped in coffee.

Alle susine e mandorle / With plums and almonds

Late summer is the time for this particular combination, but the concept carries through the seasons by varying the fruit. Use thin orange slices or pears in the winter. Turn to cherries or apricots in the spring. Arrange sliced peaches or nectarines on top in the summer.

To feed the eye as well as you feed the mouth, try using different varieties of plums in an array of colors. If you don't mind a little booze, use amaretto instead of almond extract.

Position a rack in the lower third of the oven and heat the oven to 375°F / 190°C / gas mark 5.

Stir the almond extract into the ricotta filling.

Pour the filling into the tart shell. It should come about halfway up the sides. Tap the mold on the counter a few times to level the filling.

Pit the plums and cut them each into 6 to 8 wedges. Arrange the sliced plums skin side up in concentric circles over the filling. Leave a little central circle uncovered and fill it with 1 tablespoon of the almonds. Scatter the rest of the almonds all over the tart.

Place the tart on a sheet pan and slide the pan onto the lower rack of the oven. Bake for 40 to 45 minutes, until the edges of the tart are a dull detectable brown.

Let cool before serving. Keep any leftovers covered on a cool counter or in the refrigerator for no longer than 2 days.

MAKES ONE 10-INCH / 25-CM TART; FOR 8 TO 10 PEOPLE

1 teaspoon almond extract

1½ cups / 240 g basic ricotta tart filling

One 10-inch / 25-cm pasta frolla tart shell

5 to 8 ripe but firm plums (quantity depends on size)

4 tablespoons / 25 g sliced almonds

Grated zest of ½ orange

1¼ cups / 200 g basic
ricotta tart filling if using
the jam, or 1½ cups / 240 g
if not using the jam

¼ cup / 80 g fig jam
(optional)

One 10-inch / 25-cm
pasta frolla tart shell

8 to 12 brown or green figs
(quantity depends on size)

½ cup / 70 g finely
chopped raw pistachios

Ai fichi e pistacchi / With figs and pistachio

There were three large fig trees in the garden of my childhood home. Once they started producing in August, they were relentless until mid to late October. During September peaks, Francesco Ciaccasassi, our gardener, could gather ten pounds (4.5 kilograms) in a single go. We ate them in all manners, sweet and savory. But I always favored them neat just off the branch. They were the flavor that ferried me out of golden summer days and into coppery fall sunsets.

The combination of jam and fresh fruit keeps the bottom crispier, but you can also skip the jam and add an extra ¼ cup / 40 g ricotta filling. Brown figs provide an appealing color contrast to the pistachios, but green figs will work too.

Position a rack in the lower third of the oven and heat the oven to 375°F / 190°C / gas mark 5.

Stir the orange zest into the ricotta filling.

If using the jam, spread it evenly over the bottom crust, then pour the filling into the tart shell. It should come about halfway up the sides. Tap the mold on the counter a few times to level the filling.

Stem the figs and quarter them lengthwise.

Sprinkle half of the pistachios in a circle 1 inch / 2.5 cm wide around the edge of the tart. Follow with a circle of fig wedges, alternating them skin side up and skin side down. Follow the figs with another circle 1 inch / 2.5 cm wide of the remaining pistachios. Finish with artfully arranged fig quarters in the center.

Place the tart on a sheet pan and slide the pan onto the lower rack of the oven. Bake for 40 to 45 minutes, until the edges of the tart are a dull detectable brown.

Let cool before serving. Keep any leftovers covered on a cool counter or in the refrigerator for no longer than 2 days.

SECTION IV

CARNE / MEAT

Crostini con mousse di mortadella
Crostini with mortadella mousse

Bufala, fichi e prosciutto al profumo di menta
Mint-scented buffalo mozzarella, figs, and prosciutto

Garganelli ai porri e nocciole con crumble di speck
Garganelli with leeks, hazelnuts, and speck crumble

Tagliolini all'uovo risottati con guanciale e parmigiano
One-pan tagliolini with guanciale and parmigiano

**Risotto al profumo di timo con pancetta croccante
e cipolle caramellate**
Thyme-scented risotto with crispy guanciale and
caramelized onions

Calamari ripieni di pane e 'nduja al forno
Baked calamari filled with bread and spicy Calabrian sausage

Filetto di maiale in crosta di pane condita
Pork tenderloin in seasoned bread crust

CHAPTER 9

SALUMI / CURED MEATS

The Cromwells of the pantry, working behind the scenes
to achieve greatness

Before there were cooling systems, there were pantries. The pantry of my childhood home was chilled with cross ventilation drawn straight from the underground wine cellar. Those drafts were full of centuries-old bacteria and cultures that interplayed with the provisions whose crafting clocked the seasons of our household. It was a room that felt magical to the very young me. In summer, I found respite in it from the unforgiving heat and deafening cicada song. In winter, I hid there from the boredom of homework and chores in the pages of a book. My favorite corner to curl up in was under the lanternone, a large, lantern-shaped cabinet resting on stilts with wire-mesh sides and top. It was a vantage point to catch the scent of the pig bits hooked to the top mesh. They were salumi, salt-cured, air-dried pork in whole pieces or ground sausage. Every early winter, a team of three experienced butchers and cure masters slaughtered the pigs we had raised on acorns and leftovers, then took over our kitchen for four days, at the end of which a new batch of salumi filled the aging room. The bounty left from the previous year was moved to the lanternone for my sniffing pleasure.

Half a century later, I still can't resist that scent. Salumi are a staple in my refrigerator. I initiated my son at an early age, and we still bond over them. We eat them just as they come, and love them with bread. But in an Italian kitchen, salumi have as big a role as ingredients as they have on sandwiches and platters. My grandmother Alba's secret to her legendary roast chicken? Prosciutto fat under the skin. My mother's meat loaf on steroids? Pumped by mortadella.

There is a myriad of salumi in Italy. Born out of the need to stretch the life of protein-filled foods, they eventually garnered fame and a much-deserved protagonist spot. Most of them do not leave their municipality, much less the country. Plus, for a long time, because of concerns about various swine diseases, the US Food and Drug Administration (FDA) didn't welcome Italian salumi on US shores,

with the exception of prosciutto from Parma and San Daniele. We circumvented the ban by exporting know-how and launching a thriving domestic Italian-style salumi industry. But lately, the FDA has partially revised its stance and finally opened space on market shelves to many of the extraordinary salumi made in Italy.

Growing up, one of the rites of passage from elementary to middle school was that, instead of packing a snack, your parents gave you 500 liras for a hot sfilatino—the Italian answer to baguette—stuffed with mortadella. This pink homogenized cylinder of salted, spiced, encased, and boiled pork hails from Bologna. It is inexpensive, full of flavor, and a game-changing workhorse in the kitchen. In the past, a few unscrupulous makers of mortadella have not relied on top-choice cuts and gave this cold cut a bad name. The parents of my generation of children considered mortadella a bit of a mystery meat. But today, mortadella di Bologna has been rehabilitated and has a PGI seal guaranteeing its origin and quality.

Occasional family trips to Switzerland were routed via the culturally Austrian and geographically Italian area of Alto Adige, the land of speck. This was before you could get everything everywhere, and memories of the spiced smoky ham still bring the smell of blooming pastures and the sound of my parents' laughter, at once amused and exasperated by our antics. Speck is a marriage between cultures: salt curing to the south of the production area and smoking to its north. The curing phase includes a combination of spices—like bay, juniper, coriander, red garlic, and cumin, among others—that gives speck its floral character. After they've been cured, the hams are moved between cold-smoking and air-drying rooms until they are ready to age for a minimum of twenty-two weeks.

Both pancetta and guanciale were part of the bouquet that tickled my nose during secret pantry time. They are often lumped into one, and that is not wrong. Both are salt-cured and air-dried very fatty salumi with scribbles of dark pink lean meat running along their centers. They can swoop in for each other in the kitchen. If asked to contrast them, I would say that pancetta is an urbane demagogue with a dazzling smile, while guanciale is more of a bespectacled intellectual of few but meaningful words. They both silently but surely slide in until you can't do without them. There are other macro-traits beyond personality that distinguish the two.

Pancetta is an evenly thick rectangle or a roll made with pork belly—*pancia* means "belly"—and guanciale is a tapering triangle of cured pork jowl—*guancia* is the word for "cheek." The fat of these two cuts is different. Belly fat is delicate and glossy with a pinkish tinge and an ephemeral floral quality to the nose. Jowl fat is a dull white that smells piquant and farmy; its flavor is strong and lasting. Pancetta has more lean meat. It is made throughout the country, with differences linked to the area of production. Pancetta arrotolata is rolled and typical of the north, while stesa, or "stretched," pancetta is found everywhere else. Spicing varies and can include pepper and other spices, red chili flakes, herbs, or garlic. There are two PDO-branded pancettas. The piacentina from Piacenza in Emilia-Romagna is rolled and dry cured with salt, pepper, and cloves. The calabrese from Calabria requires salt, wine vinegar, and powdered dried chili.

Guanciale is almost entirely fat and is a specialty of central Italy. It is generally cured with just salt and pepper, with the occasional addition of herbs and chili flakes. There is no protected guanciale production, maybe because of its scrappiness and humility, or the lack of a large market, or maybe because Italians know there will always be pork jowls to cure. What I know is that once you try it, your pantry will never be without it.

'Nduja is a funky, spreadable salami from Calabria, where hot chilis are as common on the table as bread and salt. Inordinate amounts of Calabrian chili account for its red-hot flavor and color. The spreadability comes from subverting the one-to-three ratio of fat to lean meat used for sliceable salami. Its funk derives from some early-on acidic

fermentation that gives it a long and stable life. 'Nduja is a tradition born out of the ingenuity of need when the poor had to find ways to stretch scarce scraps into lasting nutrition. But in the last decade or so, it has finally found the spotlight where it was always meant to live. Slightly warm, it melts into a next-level dip, and small quantities of 'nduja in a sauce, a filling, or a soup can be transformative to the flavor.

Prosciutto production is concentrated in northern and central Italy. The northern hams are variations of a common model that prefers large hind legs with surrounding fat and cures with the least possible amount of salt, resulting in what we Italians call *prosciutto dolce*—"sweet prosciutto"—think Parma, San Daniele, or Carpegna, all PDO-branded productions. Central Italian prosciutti start from legs striated with fat throughout. They rely on an abundant cure of salt and pepper. We call this *prosciutto saporito*—"savory prosciutto"—and its prime example is the PDO-labeled prosciutto toscano produced in Tuscany and Umbria.

I grew up in Umbria, where prosciutto fat is a fundamental ingredient. Our kitchen had an ongoing bin for the left-behind trimmings of prosciutto slicing, and after meals, my mom would save the fat strips my siblings separated from the red lean meat—I ate mine with cheese rinds. The fat layer all around the leg of a pig is of outstanding quality. When cured with salt and hung to slowly age for at least twelve months, it becomes exceptional. I also love to cook the lean part of prosciutto. It becomes crispy while releasing its soulful salinity to the rest of the dish.

At the Italian deli counter, mortadella is always the budget choice. Yet this humble salume is a secret weapon in the Italian kitchen. Even without revealing its presence, it elevates pasta fillings and moms' meatballs. In this recipe, it takes center stage as the protagonist of a spread tempered by cream and ricotta. I love this playful and pleasing mousse just as it is. But if you want to break the chromatic monotony, sprinkle it with a little pistachio, bring out a bright note with chives and lemon peel, or dignify it with some truffle shavings.

Crostini con mousse di mortadella
Crostini with mortadella mousse

Bring a small saucepan of water to a boil. Immerse the pistachios in the boiling water for a couple of minutes, then drain, peel, and finely chop.

Place a tight-mesh sieve over a bowl and press the ricotta through it with a rubber spatula. Combine the ricotta and mortadella in a food processor and cream into a smooth, homogeneous mixture.

Transfer the mixture to a bowl. Stir in the pistachios and parmigiano. Grate in nutmeg until you can smell it without bending over the bowl. Sprinkle in a pinch of pepper. Mix well to evenly distribute the spices. Whip the cream to soft peaks and fold it in.

Cut the baguette on a slant into slices ½ inch / 12 mm thick. Toast the slices until they are crackly and have a little color on top but are still tender inside.

Spread a generous layer of mortadella mousse on the toasted slices, and serve while the bread is still warmish.

MAKES ABOUT 2 CUPS / 290 G SPREAD

¼ cup / 30 g raw pistachios

⅓ cup / 80 g ricotta

1 cup / 180 g diced mortadella

1 tablespoon grated parmigiano reggiano

Nutmeg, for grating

Pepper

2 tablespoons heavy cream

1 baguette

In the heat of summer, while the rest of the world fawns over prosciutto and melon, I celebrate a pairing that, while less known, is eons more felicitous for my palate: figs and prosciutto. Round up the sweet and sapid coupling with the tang of buffalo mozzarella and bright mint and you will soon be asking: "Melon, who?". I hardly ever peel figs; I just wash them and rub them to a shine. But if you'd rather have skinless fruit, that works as well.

Bufala, fichi e prosciutto al profumo di menta
Mint-scented buffalo mozzarella, figs, and prosciutto

FOR 4 PEOPLE

8 figs

1 ball (8 ounces / 225 g) buffalo mozzarella (or two 4-ounce / 115-g balls)

1 mint sprig

6 slices prosciutto

Pepper

1 to 2 tablespoons extra-virgin olive oil

Flake salt

Stem the figs and quarter them lengthwise. Cut the mozzarella into 6 to 8 wedges, then cut each wedge into 2 or 3 chunks. Pick the mint leaves from the stem.

Arrange the fig quarters and mozzarella chunks on a platter. Tear the prosciutto slices into strips and drape them here and there over the platter.

Season everything with pepper to suit your taste and drizzle with the olive oil. Sprinkle a few flakes of salt on the figs and mozzarella. Tear the mint leaves into pieces and scatter them over the dish. Serve cool.

Speck hits every note: salt and smoke give it brine and wood, herbs make it floral, and spices underpin it with fragrant warmth. It is my husband's favorite among prosciutto-type salumi. I created this recipe for him. The velvety sweet of braised leeks espouses well with the speck. While I almost always encourage swapping one nut for another in a pinch, stick to hazelnuts here. They really, really work.

Garganelli ai porri e nocciole con crumble di speck
Garganelli with leeks, hazelnuts, and speck crumble

Heat the oven to 300°F / 150°C / gas mark 2.

Set a cooling rack on a sheet pan and lay the speck slices on it. Slide the pan into the oven and roast for 20 minutes, until the speck is crisp and brittle.

Meanwhile, strip off the outer layer of each leek, then cut off the root end and the top one-third of the leaves. Slice the leeks into thin rounds and leave them to float in a salad spinner filled with water, agitating them occasionally to help the grit fall away.

Lift the salad spinner basket out of the water and shake the leeks into a large frying pan. Add the oil and 1 teaspoon salt. Turn on the heat to medium-high, cover the pan, and braise the leeks for 20 to 25 minutes, until completely wilted and tender. Check periodically to ensure the leeks aren't sticking, adding a little warm water if needed.

While the leeks are braising, fill a pot with 3 quarts / 3 L water, cover it, and set it over heat to come to a boil.

When the leeks and speck are almost ready, season the water with 1½ teaspoons salt, stir in the pasta, and cover the pot. Set a timer for 3 minutes shy of the suggested cooking time. When the water comes back to a boil, uncover and adjust the heat so the water is at a lively, but not rolling, boil.

When the timer goes off, fish the pasta out of the pot with a handheld strainer and add it to the frying pan with the leeks. Raise the heat to high and add ½ cup / 120 ml of the pasta cooking water. Swirl and jostle the pan for a few minutes to finish cooking the pasta.

When the pasta is ready, finish with a drizzle of olive oil, add the hazelnuts, and toss well. Transfer to a warm serving platter and crumble the speck over it. Serve right away, with the parmigiano on the side.

FOR 4 PEOPLE

3 slices speck

2 leeks

2 tablespoons extra-virgin olive oil, plus more for finishing

Salt and pepper

1 package (8 ounces / 225 g) egg garganelli (or other dry egg pasta)

¼ cup / 25 g toasted, skinned hazelnuts, roughly chopped

¼ cup / 60 ml grated parmigiano reggiano

What is known as one-pot pasta in the United States, we Italians call pasta risottata, meaning pasta cooked with the risotto method. The technique has been around for quite some time. I learned it as a green cook back in the late 1980s. But it received renewed attention during the pandemic as we were all yearning for fast, easy, and tasty meals. It isn't always the right technique, but when skillfully applied, it can deliver insane flavors, like with this pasta.

Tagliolini all'uovo risottati con guanciale e parmigiano
One-pan tagliolini with guanciale and parmigiano

FOR 3 TO 4 PEOPLE

½ teaspoon salt

2 slices guanciale, ⅛ inch / 3 mm thick

1 package (8 ounces / 225 g) tagliolini

2 tablespoons / 60 ml grated parmigiano reggiano

Freshly ground pepper, for finishing

Pour 1 quart / 1 L water into a measuring pitcher and heat it in the microwave until hot but not boiling. Season it with ½ teaspoon salt

Stack the guanciale slices and cut them crosswise into short matchsticks.

Heat a 10- to 12-inch / 25- to 30-cm heavy-bottomed frying pan over medium-high heat until hovering your hand over it becomes uncomfortable. Add the guanciale and listen for a marked sizzle. Stir the guanciale and jostle the pan for barely a minute, just until some golden blisters appear on the surface of the meat.

Turn down the heat to low to let the guanciale render its fat without burning. In 3 to 4 minutes, when the fragrant fat pools visibly on the bottom of the pan, add the raw tagliolini and then barely cover them with the hot water. Turn the heat down until the water is at a simmer.

Swirl and jostle the pan while the tagliolini cook, adding a little more hot water if and as necessary. Tagliolini should take 4 to 5 minutes at the most to get to the al dente stage. They will absorb water while also releasing starch. The starch will bind the liquid and the guanciale fat into an emulsion that will gossamer along the pasta strands.

Dust with the parmigiano and give one last swirl to further emulsify the sauce. Finish generously with pepper, transfer to a warm platter, and serve right away with more parmigiano on the side.

This risotto requires a little planning as caramelizing onions is a long task. If you decide to embark on it, prepare a lot more onions than you need. You can freeze what you do not need in this recipe for a number of other uses. Once you have the caramelized magic, the rest of the risotto is a snap.

Risotto al profumo di timo con pancetta croccante e cipolle caramellate
Thyme-scented risotto with crispy guanciale and caramelized onions

Save 1 onion for the stock and peel the rest. Halve the onions stem to root end, then slice them into paper-thin half-moons. Heat the oil and 1½ teaspoons salt in a sauté pan over medium heat. When the fragrance of the oil wafts to your nose and hovering a hand over the pan becomes uncomfortable, stir in the onions and cook for 10 to 12 minutes, until they are translucent and lose their stiffness, stirring often to prevent sticking. Add ½ cup / 120 ml warm water to the pan and turn down the heat to low. Cover and braise the onions for 2 to 3 hours, until the onions are tobacco brown and substantially reduced in volume. Check often and add warm water as needed to keep them from sticking and burning.

Cut the saved onion in half, leaving the skin on. Fill a saucepan with 5 cups / 1.2 L water, add the onion halves, 1 of the thyme sprigs, and 2 teaspoons salt, and bring to just below the boiling point. Cover and keep hot over the lowest heat setting.

Transfer the caramelized onions to a blender or food processor and puree to a fluid, silky cream, adding some warm water if it seems too thick. Stack the pancetta slices and cut them crosswise into matchsticks. Mince the shallot and a pinch of salt into a paste. Strip the leaves off 1 of the thyme sprigs and mince them.

Heat a wide saucepan or sauté pan no more than 4 inches / 10 cm deep over medium-high heat. When hovering a hand over it becomes uncomfortable, toss in the pancetta. Let it sizzle, swirling it just until it is blistered with golden spots. Turn the heat to the lowest setting and let the pancetta render its fat. When it is crispy on the outside but still with a tender heart, remove it from the pan, leaving the fat behind. Set the pancetta aside for later use.

continued

FOR 4 PEOPLE

2½ to 3 pounds / 680 to 90 g white or yellow onions

2 tablespoons extra-virgin olive oil

Salt and pepper

3 thyme sprigs

2 slices pancetta, ⅛ inch / 3 mm thick

1 small shallot

2½ tablespoons unsalted butter, at room temperature

1 cup / 200 g rice for risotto

1 cup / 240 ml dry white wine, at room temperature

½ cup / 120 ml grated parmigiano reggiano

Risotto al profumo di timo con pancetta croccante e cipolle caramellate, continued

Add 1½ teaspoons of the butter to the pancetta fat. As soon as the butter begins to foam, add the shallot-salt paste and minced thyme and sauté, stirring often, for 2 to 3 minutes, until the shallot is quite soft, glassy, and hazy.

Stir the rice into the butter and shallot, raise the heat to medium, and set a timer for 20 minutes. Stir the rice continuously to coat it in deliciousness for 1 to 2 minutes, until it is shiny and translucent and has lost its lightly dusty smell. Raise the heat to high and pour in the wine. When the wine no longer smells acidic and caresses rather than curls your nose, add 4 cups / 950 ml of the hot salted water. It will come to a boil almost immediately. Lower the heat until the rice is at a lively bubble but not boiling. You will need to stay close to the stove, but there will be no need to stir. Just move it occasionally to check that it isn't sticking.

At minute 10, the rice grains will have grown considerably but still be completely covered in the liquid, which will be cloudy but still quite soupy.

At about minute 15, taste for salt and adjust as necessary. The liquid will be detectably starchy, and the rice will be close to the surface but barely visible. If the tips of the rice grains are peeking above the surface of the liquid, add a ladleful of the hot salted water.

At minute 18, the rice should be easily visible above the surface and the liquid tightening but still very runny. If it is too dense, add a little more hot salted water. Stay close, wooden spoon in hand.

By minute 20, the rice should be fully visible; the grains will be together but separate and can easily be moved around the pan. Stir in half of the onion puree and 2 tablespoons of the hot salted water.

Turn off the heat and vigorously stir in the remaining 2 tablespoons butter and 2 tablespoons of the parmigiano. Garnish with the pancetta bits and the last thyme sprig. Serve immediately with the remaining parmigiano and onion puree on the side.

Calamari are definitely a candidate for my last meal. I have yet to meet a dish involving them that I didn't like, though this one—created out of ingenuity and scraps for a lunch I catered on a limited budget—is a particular darling of mine and has become red hot among my students and friends. The almost entire lack of salt in this preparation is by design. The elements have deep favors that do not need coaxing or enhancing.

Calamari ripieni di pane e 'nduja al forno
Baked calamari filled with bread and spicy Calabrian sausage

Cleaning calamari is a messily relaxing business that you will want to carry out in the kitchen sink. Have three small bowls ready, one for the bodies, one for the tentacles, and the third one for the calamari refuse. Place the calamari in a colander and rinse them well. Separate the bodies from the tentacles.

To clean the bodies, dig through the inside of a body to find the feather-shaped bone and pull it all out. If the bone is not the length of the body and tapered on both ends, dive back in for the rest. Hold the calamari by the tip with one hand and run a thumb and index finger along the outside from the tip to the opening to squeeze out the gunk and guts. Repeat until all the bodies are clean.

Pick up a set of tentacles and flip it over; it will look like a bunch of flowers. You will see an opening in the center where a beak-like set of teeth is lodged. Squeeze the opening to pop it out. Turn the tentacles back over and rip any lingering gut-adjacent remnants off the top. Lastly, carefully poke a little tear on each eye with the tip of a paring knife and coax out the tiny, round crystals. Repeat with the remaining tentacles.

Return the calamari bodies and tentacles to the colander for one last quick rinse and leave them to drain while you finish prepping the rest of the ingredients.

Coarsely chop the bread. Remove the 'nduja from its casing.

FOR 6 PEOPLE

6 calamari, 6 to 7 inches / 15 to 18 cm long

2 to 3 slices day-old bread

2 ounces / 60 g packed 'nduja

1 shallot

¼ cup / 5 g loosely packed parsley leaves, plus 1 sprig

1 small orange

2 tablespoons tomato concentrate (or paste)

2 tablespoons extra-virgin olive oil

½ teaspoon salt

continued

Combine half of the tentacles, the bread, and 'nduja in a food processor and pulse until they have come together in a dense block that still has visible pieces of bread. Move the filling to a bowl.

Grate the shallot straight into the bowl on the second smallest holes of a box grater. Chop the parsley leaves finely, then toss them into the bowl. Lastly, grate the zest from half of the orange directly into the bowl. Combine everything well.

Heat the oven to 375°F / 190°C / gas mark 5.

Cut each of the remaining tentacles in half. Fill the calamari bodies with the 'nduja mixture; be careful not to pack them too fully. Secure the openings with toothpicks and affix half a tentacle to each of the toothpicks.

Add the tomato concentrate, 1 tablespoon of the olive oil, and the salt to 1 cup / 240 ml water and whisk well. Pour the mixture into a baking dish in which the calamari will fit snugly. Arrange the calamari in the dish, top them with the last parsley sprig, and drizzle with the remaining tablespoon olive oil.

Slide the baking dish into the oven and bake for 15 to 20 minutes, until the calamari change color to violet pink and no longer look slimy. Maybe a calamaro or two will burst open as the filling expands from the heat. Consider it a joyful act, one that will not at all impact the fabulousness of this dish. Serve warm.

There is an inverse proportion between how easy this unusual roast is for the cook and how much it impresses the eater. It came to life as an improvisation to make some unexpected guests feel welcome. It was such a hit that within two weeks it made it into the regular class rotation and became one of the dishes my students treasure and even pass on to their college-bound kids.

Fennel is the defining flavor of porchetta and is a very good fit for all things pork. But feel free to use different herbs. Rosemary, sage, thyme, savory, or bay would all work. You can up the garlic or eliminate it altogether. Want a kick? Add some red chili flakes. I have used duck fat when I was out of lard and have substituted pancetta for the prosciutto. In this case, reduce the amount of lard by half as pancetta is fattier than prosciutto. One last suggestion, assemble two of these, wrap the extra one tightly in plastic wrap and aluminum foil, and hold in the freezer for up to 3 months. Once thawed and roasted, it'll be as good as just made.

Filetto di maiale in crosta di pane condita
Pork tenderloin in seasoned bread crust

FOR 6 PEOPLE

1 pork tenderloin, about 1½ pounds / 680 g

2 teaspoons salt

1 baguette

1 tablespoon fennel seeds

1 teaspoon black peppercorns

1 handful wild fennel fronds (or substitute dill or farmed fennel fronds)

1 to 2 garlic cloves

¼ cup / 60 g lard

3 to 4 prosciutto slices

Heat the oven to 425° / 220°C / gas mark 7.

Sprinkle the tenderloin all over with 1 teaspoon of the salt and leave it on the counter to come to room temperature. Slit the baguette down one of the long sides, leaving the opposite side attached, and open it as if it were a book.

Heat a small frying pan over medium heat until hovering your hand over it feels uncomfortable. Toss in the fennel seeds and swirl the pan until you smell the seeds' fragrance. Pulverize the fennel seeds with the peppercorns in a spice grinder or with a mortar and pestle and pour the powder into a small bowl. Mince together the wild fennel and garlic and add to the bowl. Then add the remaining 1 teaspoon salt and stir to mix well.

Work three-fourths of the seasoning into the lard. Smear the inside of the baguette with the seasoned lard, then upholster it with the prosciutto slices.

Roll the tenderloin in the leftover seasoning and lay it in the slit bread over the prosciutto. Tighten the baguette around the meat and secure everything with butcher's twine as if tying a roast. If the baguette overshoots either tip of the meat by more than 2 inches / 5 cm, trim its ends to come closer to the tenderloin. Place the bread-covered tenderloin on a sheet pan.

Slide the pan into the oven and roast for 30 to 35 minutes, until a thermometer inserted halfway into the tenderloin registers 130°F / 55°C.

Let rest for 5 to 10 minutes, then remove the twine, cut it into slices 1½ inches / 4 cm thick, and serve.

PESCE / FISH

Burro di acciughe piccante
Spicy anchovy compound butter

Bucatini alla pasta di acciughe con olio speziato di Linda
Bucatini with anchovy paste and Linda's spiced oil

Cicorie d'inverno in salsa di acciughe
Winter chicories with anchovy dressing

Acciughe marinate
Marinated anchovies

Scaloppe di pollo alla colatura di acciughe
Chicken cutlets with anchovy colatura

CHAPTER 10

ACCIUGHE /
ANCHOVIES

You think you don't like anchovies, but you do—everybody does

Every time I start talking about anchovies, my voice goes up two octaves, I blush, and I move my hands way more than the average Italian. These tiny fish have the might to make me lose composure, logic, and thread of thought. To spare the reader an incoherently shrill page, I called the most dedicated anchovy professional I know.

Giulio Giordano lives and works in Cetara, a one-main-road-to-the-tiny-port kind of town toward the southern end of the Amalfi Coast on the Gulf of Salerno. Cetara has been the fishing center of the Amalfi Coast nervous system since it was settled at the tail end of the first millennium CE. Giulio and his brother still carry on the anchovy business, Nettuno, their father started in 1950. They work in the same three rooms where their father worked, and they are the last artisanal outfit still left by the port. While others have moved to larger and more efficient facilities, they have made the choice to keep their business rigorously artisanal.

Anchovies, Giulio tells me, are fished at night in spring and summer. In August, the schools go out to deep, rough waters for some R&R—romancing and reproducing—and stay away until the early spring. Within a few hours of being caught, the fish are gutted and beheaded. Then they are tossed into vats of brine for twenty-four hours to dehydrate by 70 percent. On day two, the anchovies are tightly layered head to tail in chestnut-wood barrels called terzigni—loosely translatable as "little thirds" because they are one-third the size of a standard wine barrel. The anchovy layers are separated by layers of rock salt. A cover is placed in direct contact with the top layer and weighed down to press the anchovies for six months of ripening.

Once they are ready, they can be sold as they are or rinsed and repacked in oil. Anchovy fillets in oil are ready to eat or use in a recipe that calls for them. But whole anchovies packed in salt must be carefully rinsed and thoroughly cleaned first. The salt anchovies will last for a very long time without drying or oxidizing. Anchovies in oil also last for a while, but they can dry out, and the oil can become rancid.

Anchovies can also be bought as a paste, a tube of which is always in my refrigerator as I grew up on it. My mother considered bread, butter, and anchovy paste a dreamy breakfast when dipped in caffelatte, and she was right. Anchovy paste is a fast flavor enhancer, and as long as the tube is resealed, it will stay good for months and months. I had a colleague long ago who mixed it with a little mayonnaise, a touch of garlic, a sprinkle of lemon juice, and olive oil to make a fabulous Caesar dressing.

Not all anchovies are created equal according to Giulio, and if you try anchovies from Cetara, you will agree. The depth and high salinity of the Amalfi Coast impacts the phytoplankton eaten by the anchovies and makes them quite minerally and low fat. The fish's characteristics and centuries of passed-down artisanal wisdom are what set these anchovies apart.

Cetara is also the birthplace of colatura di alici, a by-product of preserving discovered by local monks in the twelfth century. Colatura is the filtered drip that leaks from the ripening anchovies, an amber-colored liquid whose aroma and flavor are so intense they will shut down any other stimuli. It takes fifty-five pounds (twenty-five kilograms) of anchovies to make three quarts (three liters) of colatura. But just a few drops over a vegetable, in salad dressing, on pasta, or in a sauce bring out all your food has to offer.

If just the sound of the word anchovy has you hot and bothered, this is the recipe for you. It is embarrassingly easy to make for the amount of joy it delivers to the taste buds. Spread it on toast, dab it on a steak, slather it on potatoes, melt it over greens, or serve it to a chosen few with toasted bread alongside a spritz. The ingredients in the recipe are calibrated for a stick of butter, but once you taste it, you will want to have it on hand all the time. Make a whole pound / 450 g, pack it in small logs, and keep it in the freezer. And play with this recipe: use scallions or garlic instead of shallot, swap out mint for basil or chervil, use a lemon or kumquat for tartness in lieu of a lime, sweeten it with a mandarin, or tame the heat by using a pepper sweeter than cayenne.

Burro di acciughe piccante
Spicy anchovy compound butter

Cut the butter into tablespoons. Lay the anchovy fillets on a paper towel to drain the oil. Grate enough of the shallot on the second smallest holes of a box grater to make 1 tablespoon. Grate the zest from half of the lime. Roughly chop the mint.

Combine the butter, anchovies, shallot, lime zest, mint, and a pinch of cayenne in the food processor and run it until the mixture is a cream. Taste it for spiciness and add cayenne if you fancy a little more heat.

Spatula the butter onto a piece of parchment paper and push it toward one end of the paper, using the spatula to give it the rough shape of a log. Roll the paper tightly around the butter and smooth it into a neatly formed log with a diameter of about 1½ inches / 4 cm. Twist the ends as if you were wrapping a hard candy and refrigerate.

The butter will keep for 3 to 4 weeks in the refrigerator and up to 6 months in the freezer.

**MAKES ABOUT
6 OUNCES / 170 G**

1 stick / 4 ounces / 115 g unsalted butter

10 anchovy fillets packed in oil

1 shallot

1 lime

10 to 12 mint leaves

Cayenne pepper

My friend Linda Tay hails from Malaysia, and she's of Chinese descent. She teaches the cooking of her own culture and country. Through years of overlapping career paths, we have bonded over our deep understanding of the social and cultural implications of food and our insatiable curiosity for all kinds of cuisines, including each other's. In exchange for my famed salsa verde recipe, she unlocked the secret to her legendary Sichuan red chili oil. Linda uses high-quality vegetable oil, like rice bran, but she gave me her blessing when I told her I wanted to use extra-virgin olive oil, though she suggested that I select a kind with a floral flavor profile. I chose one from Liguria. Once the spiced oil is ready and cooled down, you can store it in a tightly sealed jar in a cool, dry place or in the refrigerator. You will soon find that its uses extend way beyond this pasta.

Bucatini alla pasta di acciughe con olio speziato di Linda
Bucatini with anchovy paste and Linda's spiced oil

For the spiced oil

2 tablespoons Sichuan peppercorns

1 cup / 240 ml light and floral extra-virgin olive oil

½ cup / 95 g dried small whole chilis

½-inch / 12-mm piece ginger, unpeeled and lightly smashed

1 scallion, white part only

1 teaspoon whole cloves

¼ teaspoon cumin seeds

¼ teaspoon fennel seeds

1 piece cassia bark, or 1-inch / 2.5-cm piece cinnamon stick

1 star anise pod

1 black cardamom pod, or 2 or 3 green cardamom pods

Start with the spiced oil. Gently toast the Sichuan peppercorns in a dry saucepan over medium-low heat until their fragrance wafts to your nostrils. Stay close and be mindful not to burn them. When the peppercorns are ready, remove half of them from the pan.

Add the olive oil, whole chilis, ginger, scallion, cloves, cumin and fennel seeds, cassia bark, star anise, and cardamom to the pan. Leave it over the lowest heat setting for about 40 minutes, until the scallion is wrinkly and golden.

While the oil is heating, grind the other half of the Sichuan peppercorns in a spice grinder or with a mortar and pestle. Place them in a heatproof jar and add the chili powder, chili flakes, and salt.

When the oil is ready, remove it from the heat and let it cool to 275°F / 140°C, then strain it through a tight-mesh strainer into the prepared jar. You can discard what is left behind in the strainer. The oil will need to steep for at least 2 hours before it is ready for use, but with time the flavors will bloom in intensity. You should have 1 cup / 240 ml.

continued

Bucatini alla pasta di acciughe con olio speziato di Linda, continued

While the oil is steeping, prepare the bucatini. Fill a tall pot with 4 quarts / 1 L water, cover it, and set it over heat to come to a boil.

When the water is boiling, season it with 1 teaspoon salt, drop in the bucatini, stir, and cover the pot. Set a timer for 3 minutes shy of the suggested cooking time. When the water starts to boil again, remove the cover and adjust the heat so the water is at a lively, but not rolling, boil.

While the pasta cooks, smash and peel the garlic clove and put it into a 12-inch / 30-cm frying pan with 3 tablespoons of the spiced oil. Turn on the heat to low and wait by the pan until tight bubbles are sizzling around the garlic clove and its fragrance billows to your nose. Turn the clove over to blister on the other side then discard it. Add the anchovy paste and swirl it with a wooden spoon to dilute it in the oil. Turn off the heat.

If you are using a salt-packed anchovy, thoroughly rinse off the salt. Slit the belly then gently pry it open, leaving the back attached. Rinse out the gunk and guts. Carefully separate the spine from the flesh and snap it off right before the tail. If using oil-packed anchovy fillets, no prep is necessary.

The timer should go off shortly. When it does, fish the bucatini out of the water with tongs and transfer them to the pan with the oil and anchovy paste. Raise the heat to high and add 1 cup / 240 ml of the pasta cooking water. Swirl and jostle the pan often to emulsify the starch and fat into a gossamer sauce along the strands of pasta, adding small spoonfuls of cooking water if and as needed.

When the bucatini are al dente, finish with another 1 to 2 tablespoons of the spiced oil and transfer to a warm serving platter. Spoon out some of the pepper mixture from the bottom of your oil jar and drizzle it over the pasta. Garnish with the whole anchovy and serve right away.

1 tablespoon Korean chili powder

1½ teaspoons red chili flakes

1 teaspoon salt

For the bucatini for 5 to 6 people

1 teaspoon salt

1 package (1 pound / 450 g) bucatini

1 garlic clove

Spiced oil as needed

1 tablespoon anchovy paste

1 whole anchovy packed in salt, or 2 anchovy fillets packed in oil

This salad is a classic on my Christmas table. If I can find them, I use puntarelle, as per the custom of the Roman Christmases of my childhood. Puntarelle are the tips of the crunchy heart that forms inside a head of overgrown chicory. If they are unavailable, I will use a mix of brightly colored radicchio varieties. The acid-to-fat ratio in the dressing follows my mother's, but I use lemon instead of vinegar as I prefer it, and I keep the garlic scant. To push it into adult dinner-party territory, I add some pine nuts and currants.

Cicorie d'inverno in salsa di acciughe
Winter chicories with anchovy dressing

FOR 6 PEOPLE

2 heads winter chicory (any kind of radicchio, escarole, or frisée)

2 tablespoons dried currants

2 tablespoons pine nuts

6 anchovy fillets packed in oil

1 lemon

½ garlic clove

Extra-virgin olive oil as needed

1 or 2 pinches of red chili flakes

Salt

Clean and separate the chicory leaves and tear them by hand into pieces that can be manageably eaten. Drop the leaves into a salad spinner and rinse two or three times until all the dirt is gone. Submerge the clean green leaves in water, toss 8 to 10 ice cubes into the spinner, and leave the salad to crisp while you ready the rest of the ingredients.

Soak the currants in hot water. Heat a small frying pan over medium heat until hovering your hand over it feels quite uncomfortable. Toss in the pine nuts and turn off the heat. Swirl the pan to sweat and lightly toast the nuts.

Chop the anchovies roughly. Grate 1 ½ teaspoons zest from the lemon, then juice the lemon and measure how much juice it yields. Put the anchovies, lemon zest and juice, and the garlic in a blender or small food processor.

Pour three times the amount of lemon juice in olive oil into a cup. Start the blender and slowly stream in the olive oil. You will yield a dense, lovely vinaigrette. Taste and adjust with salt if necessary. You can also do this by hand with a small whisk if you do not have an electric-powered device.

Drain the chicories and spin them three or four times, pouring out the moisture that gathers at the bottom between one cycle and the next. Move the dry leaves to a salad bowl and sprinkle them with the chili flakes and 1 teaspoon salt. Toss well.

Drain and squeeze the currants and add them to the salad bowl along with the toasted pine nuts.

Pour 3 to 4 tablespoons / 45 to 60 ml of the dressing along the side of the salad bowl, then toss with salad servers or clean hands until all the leaves are coated. Add more dressing if needed, keeping in mind that the leaves should glisten, not drip. Store any extra dressing for your next salad.

Once or twice a year my father came home with a one-kilo jar of anchovies in salt. Alberta Mezzetti, his housekeeper, stopped whatever she was doing to tend to the tiny fish. She summarily rinsed two-thirds of them and repacked them in fresh salt to keep for the pantry. The rest would be processed for shorter-term consumption, and be kept in the refrigerator readily available as snacks or starters. Below is a riff on her technique. The red onion and chili are my additions, and Alberta would use parsley not mint. The lemon is a way to cut the sometimes-overpowering saltiness. I serve these anchovies as an aperitivo with warm crusty bread or crackers. Whatever is left over, you can toss into a salad.

Acciughe marinate
Marinated anchovies

Slice the red onion into thin scythes, drop them into a bowl, and sprinkle them with the vinegar. Toss 3 or 4 ice cubes into the bowl and cover everything with water.

Working with one at a time, thoroughly rinse the salt off of each anchovy. Slit the belly then gently pry it open, leaving the back attached. Rinse out the gunk and guts. Carefully separate the spine from the flesh and snap it off right before the tail.

Give the anchovies one last rinse, shake off the excess water, and lay them on a plate, alternating them head to tail. Pat the little fish dry.

Douse the anchovies with the juice of the lemon half. Sprinkle them with the chili flakes and generously drizzle them with the olive oil.

Lift the onion scythes out of the bowl and shake off the excess water. Distribute them over the anchovies.

Stack the mint leaves, roll them up tightly lengthwise, and cut them crosswise into thin ribbons. Scatter the mint over the anchovies and serve.

FOR 4 PEOPLE

1 small wedge red onion

2 tablespoons red or white vinegar

12 whole anchovies packed in salt

½ lemon

1 teaspoon red chili flakes

3 to 4 tablespoons extra-virgin olive oil

8 to 10 mint leaves

There is a funny story to this dish. It saw the light at the tail end of the third photo shoot for this very book; we were all tired and hungry, and I mindlessly threw it together from whatever ingredients on my counter already had their beauty shot taken. The umami of colatura surfing on the fat waves of butter over a simple chicken breast silenced the room. Until three voices demanded in unison that the recipe be included in the book.

This chicken can be a super-fast dinner if you have a butcher who will cut and pound the chicken cutlets for you—in which case you can skip the first step. But don't fret, the recipe is simple enough even without a friendly butcher. It is just a bit more time-consuming.

Scaloppe di pollo alla colatura di acciughe
Chicken cutlets with anchovy colatura

FOR 4 PEOPLE

2 boneless, skinless chicken breasts, or 8 small chicken cutlets

Salt

1½ tablespoons all-purpose flour (or cornstarch for gluten-free)

1 dill sprig

1 tablespoon extra-virgin olive oil

3 tablespoons unsalted butter

4 tablespoons / 60 ml anchovy colatura

2 tablespoons lemon juice

4 thin lemon peel strips, about 1 inch / 2.5 cm long

1 teaspoon cracked pink pepper

Salt

Sharpen your knife then slice each chicken breast at a slant along the grain into 4 cutlets. Cover the cutlets with parchment paper and pound them one at a time by sliding a meat mallet from the center out toward the edges until the cutlet is evenly flattened to about ⅛ inch / 3 mm thick. Dust the cutlets on both sides with the flour, shaking off the excess.

Pick the dill tips.

Heat the olive oil in a large nonstick frying pan over medium heat until its fragrance reaches your nose. Add 1 tablespoon of the butter. When the butter has melted and is foamy in the center and beginning to separate at the edges, lay in the chicken in a single layer. If the cutlets do not fit in one layer, you can split them in two batches. Cook for about 3 minutes per side, turning only once. The cutlets will get some golden crusty spots. Move the chicken out of the pan with tongs and onto a warm platter, then cover with aluminum foil to keep hot.

Right away toss the remaining 2 tablespoons butter, the colatura, lemon juice, the lemon peel strips, and half of the dill tips into the frying pan and whisk together until emulsified. Sample to make sure the saltiness is suited to your taste; if it is overwhelming, you can tame it with a little more lemon juice.

Pour the sauce over the chicken and garnish with the remaining dill and the pink pepper. Taste the sauce and adjust salt if needed. Serve right away while still quite hot.

Bastoncini di pesce per intenditori
Gourmand fish sticks

Corzetti al baccalà e funghi
Corzetti with salt cod and mushrooms

Riso freddo con baccalà e pistacchi
Cold rice with salt cod and pistachios

Baccalà alla parmigiana
Lemon and garlic–scented salt cod casserole with grana

Baccalà in insalata
Steamed salt cod with heirloom tomatoes and red onions

CHAPTER 11

BACCALÀ / SALT COD

The best kept secret on the Italian pescatarian table

I must preface this chapter by saying that while my love for baccalà is unabated, I have expanded my knowledge to understand that the long history of salt cod as a food source and trade good comes with some baggage of environmental and human exploitation. You can garner a full understanding from Mark Kurlansky's fascinating 1997 book, *Cod: A Biography of the Fish That Changed the World.* Today, when I buy and cook baccalà, I am mindful of the sustainability of its sourcing, and I hold its past role as a cheap staple to feed oppressed populations as a reminder that we all must continue to strive to bring equity into our food system. Thank you for listening.

Excepting Wikipedia, all sources I checked agree that Italy is seventy-third in size among the countries of the world but jumps to an impressive fourteenth place when it comes to the length of our coastline. And that spatial relationship explains why fish eating is a religion in Italy. We have opinions on what fresh fish should taste, look, feel, sound, and smell like and from where it should come. We have a fishmonger on the list of trusted professionals to call us when sea urchins are in season or a wild sea bass appears on their counter. But for all the care, mind, and insistence we place on how fresh and local our fish must be, there is an imported secret on our pescatarian table: baccalà—aka salt cod—Atlantic cod preserved with salt and air dried. Indeed, Italy is the third-largest consumer of salt cod in the world, trailing only Brazil and Portugal.

This northern European specialty came to Italian tables via the trade ways of Venice between the fifteenth and sixteenth centuries. Long shelf life and low price soon turned it into a popular staple throughout the peninsula, where it was interpreted in a myriad of local declensions.

Gadus morhua—the scientific name for Atlantic cod—is fished and cured all along the North Sea and the Atlantic, but the two main areas of salt cod production are Norway and Canada. The Norwegian salt cod is highly prized by chefs and home cooks alike. Its flesh is thick and flaky with a delicate and unmistakable flavor. It is also way more expensive than its Canadian counterpart and not as easily sourced.

The more readily available Canadian variety is still delicious but with a more marked fishiness and a less palate-friendly texture. It can be found in specialty shops, like Italian delis and Mexican bodegas, either in whole sides or in one-pound (450-gram) skinless and boneless fillets packed in wooden boxes. Occasionally, I have found those same boxes in high-end supermarkets.

A handful of family businesses of Portuguese descent across the United States carry the meatier and more prized Norwegian salt cod. You can order it online and will have to select among a number of cuts, as the flavors and texture change as you move along toward the tail.

Loins are the choice cut, taken not too far below the gills where the body is at its widest and thickest. The bigger the cod, the meatier the loins. They are best for roasting or grilling, preparations that call for a whole piece of fish. Above the loins live the necks, and since I find relish in the overlooked, I much favor them. They are ugly enough that placing them on a plate feels almost impolite, but their substance is so full of flavor that form is easily forgotten. They are my go-to cut for any baccalà dish. The pieces below the loins tend to have less flake and more string but still deliver taste. They're fit for preparations like a stew where the baccalà becomes undone or for deep-frying. Last but not least are the belly bits that are left behind after trimming. They are fatty and tender and the most inexpensive option. They can be desalted very quickly and are ideal for sauces and for whipping or grinding.

Whatever you buy, proper soaking and desalting are critical. Baccalà that isn't properly desalted can be inedible. My mother taught me that it is better to soak to the point where you will need to season it again during cooking. Instructions on how to desalt baccalà properly are on the following page. They are not difficult, but you should follow them closely.

HOW TO PROPERLY SOAK AND DESALT BACCALÀ

Rinse the excess salt off the baccalà and place it in a container that allows some space for it to swell as it reconstitutes. Fill the container with water to cover the fish generously and leave it soaking for at least 2 and up to 5 days. The exact time is predicated on both the thickness of the piece and how long the fish has been preserved.

Change the soaking water three times a day. I soak my cod at room temperature, but if your kitchen is warm and you don't have enough space in the refrigerator, add fresh ice cubes every time you change the water.

Testing if the desalting is complete changes according to the size of the piece. Thin chunks of fairly even thickness are ready in a couple of days. Just pinch off a piece to chew—it should taste ready to be seasoned again. Thick cuts, especially the gorgeous loins, might taste like they are ready on the surface but can still pack a punch of salt in their inner layers. To avoid surprises, grab a wooden skewer and pierce the baccalà all the way to the center. Keep the skewer there for 10 to 15 seconds, then retract it and lick it. If the salinity is marked, then continue soaking. But if the taste of salt is faint, the baccalà is ready to be cooked.

I was eleven the first time I discovered frozen fish sticks. It was in Canterbury, England, during an English as a second language summer program. I was smitten. Much to my mother's dismay, I kept asking for them when I got home. To set me back on the path of good eating, she hooked me on the joys of deep-fried baccalà. It worked. There are different ways to deep-fry baccalà, from a coat of flour all the way to a cocoon of bread dough. This is a quick in-between version.

Bastoncini di pesce per intenditori
Gourmand fish sticks

Soak and desalt the baccalà as directed on page 228.

Sift together the flour and baking powder into a bowl and stir in 1 teaspoon salt.

Pour 1½ cups / 350 ml of the sparkling water into a bowl and start whisking in the flour by the handful, continuing until the batter is lump-free, glossy, and has reached a medium-dense consistency. To test if the batter is the right density, dip the whisk all the way in and lift it out. The batter should fall back into the bowl in a continuous ribbon, and it should "write" on the surface: a scribble should remain visible for about 2 seconds and then make a slight parting when it sinks back in. If the batter is too loose, add flour; if it is too dense, thin it with sparkling water. Cover and refrigerate the batter until needed.

Pour the oil to a depth of 2 inches / 5 cm into a deep sauté pan and heat to 340°F / 170°C on a thermometer. If you do not have a thermometer, you can test the temperature by dropping a small cube of bread into the oil. If the oil is hot enough, the bread will not sink and will emit a faint sizzle and release lots of lively bubbles.

While the oil is heating, remove the skin and bones from the baccalà and divide it into 8 pieces weighing 2 to 3 ounces / 60 to 90 g each. Pat the pieces very dry so the batter will stick.

Set a cooling rack over a sheet pan and place it close to the pan with the oil. Cut the lemon into wedges.

continued

FOR 4 PEOPLE

1 piece baccalà neck,
1 to 1½ pounds / 450 to 680 g

2 cups / 280 g
all-purpose flour

½ teaspoon
baking powder

Salt

2 cups / 475 ml
sparkling water

Vegetable oil,
for deep-frying

1 lemon

Bastoncini di pesce per intenditori, continued

When the oil has reached temperature, take the batter out of the fridge and drop all the baccalà pieces into the bowl.

Dredge the first piece through the batter until it is completely coated with a compact and thickish layer of batter. Some batter will inevitably drip away, but it should not slide off the surface of the fish.

This next step is very important for safety. Hold the battered baccalà piece by one end and carefully dip about 1 inch / 2.5 cm of the other end into the hot oil, then let it go so it slides in without splashing. Repeat with another 2 pieces.

Deep-fry the baccalà pieces for 7 to 10 minutes, turning the heat up or down to stay within 10°F / 5°C of the initial temperature and periodically flipping them to give them an even and deep gold color. Lift the fish sticks from the oil with a slotted spoon, let the oil drip back into the pan for a few seconds, and then place them on the rack to drain. Repeat in batches until you have fried all the baccalà.

Sprinkle with salt while still warm and serve with the lemon wedges on the side.

Ligurian corzetti are pasta disks embossed with various images. They are at once slithery and firm and have a way of folding around the tongue and encasing the sauce elements close to the taste buds. However suited they are to this recipe, they aren't easy to find, not even in Italy. You can substitute another short pasta that can cradle the bits of fish and mushrooms, like orecchiette or shells. Rosemary rounds out the wintry character of this dish, but its medicinal undertone can become overpowering, so I extract its essence by letting it infuse the cooking water and the olive oil, then discard it.

Corzetti al baccalà e funghi
Corzetti with salt cod and mushrooms

FOR 6 PEOPLE

1½ cups / 200 g baccalà bits and flakes

½ ounce / 15 g dried porcini, or 8 ounces / 225 g fresh porcini

2 rosemary sprigs, plus a few tips for garnishing

12 ounces / 340 g fresh king trumpet mushrooms

1 small shallot

3 tablespoons extra-virgin olive oil, plus more for finishing

Salt

Red chili flakes

1 package (1 pound / 450 g) corzetti

Soak and desalt the baccalà as directed on page 228.

If you are using dried porcini, rehydrate them in warm water.

Fill a pot with 3 quarts / 3 L water and set it over heat to come to a boil. Rub 1 rosemary sprig between your palms, drop it into the water, and cover the pot.

While the water heats, wipe the king trumpets clean with a paper towel, trim the very bottom of the stems, halve them from cap to stem, and then thinly slice them crosswise. If using fresh porcini, do the same with them. Grate the shallot on the second smallest holes of a box grater. If using dried porcini, they should be rehydrated by now, so drain and rinse them.

Pour 2 tablespoons of the olive oil into a large frying pan. Rub the remaining rosemary sprig between your palms and drop it into the pan. Warm slowly over medium-low heat until you smell the oil and rosemary without bending over the stove. Get rid of the rosemary, raise the heat to medium-high, and add the bits of salt cod. Sauté quickly for 3 to 4 minutes, just until the cod is shiny with oil and coated in flavor. Transfer the fish to a plate with a slotted spoon.

continued

Add the remaining 1 tablespoon olive oil to the pan. Toss in the shallot and all the mushrooms, add ½ teaspoon salt, and sauté the mushrooms until they are visibly wilted and releasing moisture. Reduce the heat to medium-low, cover, and cook for 12 to 15 minutes, occasionally checking for moisture in the bottom of the pan. If needed, add a bit of warm water to prevent sticking.

The water should be boiling by now. Discard the rosemary and season the water with 1½ tablespoons salt. Stir in the corzetti, cover the pot, and set a timer for 3 minutes shy of the suggested cooking time. When the water starts to boil again, remove the cover and adjust the heat so the water is at a lively, but not rolling, boil.

Uncover the mushrooms, return the sautéed baccalà bits to the pan, and keep cooking over medium to low heat while the pasta is boiling. Taste and adjust salt as needed and season with red chili flakes to suit your palate.

When the timer goes off, fish the pasta out of the water with a handheld strainer and add it to the pan with the mushrooms. Raise the heat to high, add ½ cup / 120 ml of the pasta cooking water, and swirl and jostle the pan for 2 to 3 minutes to finish cooking the corzetti, adding a little more cooking water if needed.

Finish with a thread of olive oil, toss well, and transfer to a warm shallow serving bowl. Garnish with the rosemary tips and serve hot.

There was so much happening when the package was delivered that I didn't notice just how brilliant the green of the pistachios was, nor how thrilling a chromatic combination it made with the basket of Meyer lemons from our friend Hasta's garden. When I did, all other dinner plans were suspended. If we eat with our eyes first, then I was bound for a treat. I happened to have some poached baccalà on hand that night, and this dish was born. I have since made it in a pinch using salt cod packed in oil with very good results.

Riso freddo con baccalà e pistacchi
Cold rice with salt cod and pistachios

Soak and desalt the baccalà as directed on page 228.

Fill a saucepan with 1 quart / 1 L water and set it on the stove to bring to a boil. Rinse the rice in a colander until the water runs clear. Season the boiling water with 1½ teaspoons salt and stir the rice into the boiling water. Lower the heat to a simmer, cover, and set a timer for 3 to 4 minutes shy of the suggested cooking time.

While the rice cooks, prepare the rest of the ingredients. Line a steamer basket with parchment paper, place the baccalà on it, and set the basket over water in a saucepan. Bring the water to a boil, turn down the heat to medium, cover, and steam for 10 to 15 minutes, until the cod is glossy, tender, and flakes easily. When cool enough to handle, remove any skin and bones, then separate the flesh into flakes.

Grate 1 teaspoon zest from the lemon, cut 2 thin slices for decoration, then juice the rest of the lemon.

Select 3 or 4 mint leaf tips for garnishing. Stack the remaining leaves, roll them up tightly lengthwise, and cut them crosswise into thin ribbons. Roughly chop the pistachios.

When the timer goes off, sample a couple of rice grains. They should be cooked but with a perceptible bite, tender but not soft. If needed, cook the rice a little longer. Otherwise, drain it and quickly rinse under room-temperature running water. Shake off any excess water and pour the rice into a serving bowl.

continued

FOR 6 PEOPLE

1 baccalà loin, about
1 pound / 450 g

1½ cups / 300 g medium-
or long-grain rice

Salt

1 Meyer lemon (or use
a regular lemon)

1 cup / 20 g loosely
packed mint or basil leaves

½ cup / 60 g shelled
raw pistachios

Red chili flakes

Extra-virgin olive oil
as needed

Riso freddo con baccalà e pistacchi, continued

Add the baccalà flakes, lemon zest, mint ribbons, and most of the chopped pistachios. Season with the lemon juice and red chili flakes to suit your taste. Toss well.

Generously douse with olive oil and toss again. Taste and adjust salt and chili flakes to suit your palate.

Dust with the remaining pistachios and garnish with the mint tips. Halve the lemon slices and artfully arrange them over the rice. Serve at room temperature.

Leftovers should be taken out of the refrigerator 10 to 15 minutes before eating and revived with a few drops of lemon juice and a drizzle of olive oil.

Throughout her eighty-plus years of living, my aunt Marzia never met a cliché she was afraid of bashing. When she served me a casserole of salt cod layered with young grana padano, she confirmed my belief and spurred my battle against the idea that fish and cheese do not play well together. I tweaked the taste memory to include a few flavor counterpoints and liquid-thickening techniques, and Aunt Donatella said she actually likes mine better than her sister Marzia's, though that will have to remain in the annals of family secrets. While this is a super-easy dish to assemble and even easier to love, it requires a bit of planning as the fish needs an extra day of soaking in milk after the two or three days it will have spent in water. You can, however, assemble the casserole the day before you bake and serve it.

Baccalà alla parmigiana
Lemon and garlic–scented salt cod casserole with grana

Soak and desalt the baccalà as directed on page 228.

The day before assembling the casserole, strip off any skin from the baccalà and tweeze out any bones. Cut the flesh into slices ⅛ inch / 3 mm thick and lay them in a sealable container. Submerge the slices in the milk, then seal the container and refrigerate overnight.

Zest the lemon into a small bowl. Chop the parsley finely and mince the garlic into a paste. Combine the zest, parsley, and garlic. If you have opted for black pepper or chili flakes, use it to season the zest, parsley, and garlic mixture, adjusting the quantity according to how spicy you enjoy your food. If you are using fresh chilis, slit them lengthwise, scrape out the seeds, and mince the flesh, then add it to the zest mixture.

Reserve 1 cup / 240 ml of the milk in which you soaked the baccalà, then drain the fish in a colander. Shake the colander well to eliminate surplus liquid. Pat the fish dry with paper towels and leave it in the colander. Tip the flour over the colander. Swirl and jostle the colander to coat the fish evenly and lightly.

FOR 6 PEOPLE

1 baccalà loin or neck, about 1 pound / 450 g

4 cups / 950 ml whole milk

1 lemon

1 cup / 20 g loosely packed parsley leaves

1 garlic clove

Black pepper or red chili flakes, 2 fresh Thai chilis, or 1 fresh árbol chili

¼ cup / 35 g all-purpose flour

2 tablespoons unsalted butter, softened into a pomade

½ cup / 60 g unseasoned dried breadcrumbs

½ cup / 120 ml grated grana padano

Toasted thickly sliced crusty bread, for serving

continued

Brush the bottom and sides of an 8-by-10-inch / 20-by-25-cm broiler-safe baking dish (or an oval or round one of similar volume) with 1 tablespoon of the butter, then dust it with half of the breadcrumbs. Twist and twirl the dish to lightly carpet it with the crumbs.

Heat the oven to 350° / 180°C / gas mark 4.

To assemble the casserole, start with a layer of fish, followed by a dusting of the grana padano and then of the spicy parsley, garlic, and zest mixture. Continue layering until you have made your way through the fish, cheese, and zest mince, finishing with a dusting of cheese. Pour the reserved milk all over and gently shake the dish to make sure the milk finds its way into the casserole's nooks and crannies. Dust with the other half of the breadcrumbs and dot with the remaining 1 tablespoon butter.

Slide the dish into the oven and bake for 35 to 40 minutes, until the milk is bubbling. Place the casserole under the broiler for a few minutes, just enough to get a few crusty, light golden spots. Let rest for 5 to 10 minutes, then serve it flanked by thick slices of lightly toasted crusty bread, as there will be some runny deliciousness to sop up.

The beauty of baccalà is that it has no fixed place in time. It moves through the year dressed by the flavors we crave in each season. In this simple recipe, wedges of heirloom tomatoes clothe my overlooked hero in swaths of summer red.

Season the tomatoes separately with oregano and with salt and pepper to suit your taste. As for the fish, if it is properly soaked, it will not need any salt, but you can add a stingy pinch of dried oregano and a few turns of a pepper grinder if you like. If the baccalà is a little too salty for your taste, sprinkle it with some red wine vinegar. Feel free to add a tender herb, like basil, cilantro, or mint.

Baccalà in insalata
Steamed salt cod with heirloom tomatoes and red onions

Soak and desalt the baccalà as directed on page 228.

Line a steamer basket with parchment paper, place the baccalà on it, and set the basket over water in a saucepan. Bring the water to a boil, turn down the heat to medium, cover, and steam for 10 to 15 minutes, until the cod is glossy, tender, and flakes easily. When cool enough to handle, remove any skin and bones, then separate the flesh into flakes.

While the baccalà is steaming, slice the onion half into scythes ⅛ inch / 3 mm thick along the stem-to-root meridians and put them into a bowl. Add 6 to 8 ice cubes and cold water to cover and leave to soak to crisp and tame some pungency.

Cut the tomatoes into wedges that are sizable but still manageable for gracious eating. Place them in a bowl and season with 1 teaspoon salt, pepper to taste, and the oregano. Toss well and drizzle with 3 tablespoons of the olive oil. Taste and adjust the oil, salt, and pepper to suit your palate.

Remove any skin and bones from the baccalà and flake it into the tomato bowl while still warm. Lift the onion slices out of the bowl and shake off the excess water, then scatter them over the salad. Drizzle with a little olive oil for shine and serve.

FOR 6 PEOPLE

1 baccalà loin, about 1 pound / 450 g

½ small red onion

1½ pounds / 680 g heirloom tomatoes

Salt and pepper

1 teaspoon dried oregano

3 to 4 tablespoons extra-virgin olive oil, plus more for finishing

Vellutata di sedano di Verona con bottarga
Celery root soup with bottarga

Uova in crema alla bottarga di tonno
Creamed eggs with tuna bottarga

Spaghetti alla bottarga della zia Milla
Aunt Milla's spaghetti with bottarga

Filetto di maiale con carciofi e bottarga di muggine
Pork tenderloin with artichokes and mullet bottarga

Trofie con ricotta e bottarga di muggine al profumo di arancio
Trofie with orange-scented ricotta and mullet bottarga

Cannellini e bottarga
Cannellini and bottarga

CHAPTER 12

BOTTARGA / SALT CURED FISH ROE

The ineffable essence of the sea

My mother held my hand as we walked through the stifling and pungent back shop of her favorite fishmonger in Orbetello, on the southern Tuscan coast. It was my seventh late September, and the air and sun tasted especially sweet when we walked out and into a courtyard. The breeze from the lagoon we were overlooking brought a flutter to the broken heart–shaped flaps hanging inside a wire-mesh cabinet. Those broken hearts are why we are here, and I can't pry my eyes off their color, like that of a rusty sunset. I see my mother's hand sliding over them until she settles on the one she deems worthy—mostly a matter of size given that the family table always has space for one more. *"Questa è la bottarga amore,"*—"This is *bottarga*, love,"—she says to me, then asks the fishmonger to explain how it's made. We shaved it over buttered toast with lemon as soon as we got home and later grated it into freckles over spaghetti with olive oil and parsley. It was unlike anything I had tried before. It tasted like the sea, like salt and wind, like the inside of shells, like I imagined Hans Christian Andersen's The Little Mermaid to taste if I could eat that tale. Fifty years later, *bottarga* is a fixture of my pantry, and I am still swept away to that moment every time I eat it.

But what is *bottarga*? As that long-ago fisherman explained to me, *bottarga* is the roe sac of certain kinds of fish that is carefully extracted so as not to tear its membrane, then cured with salt, pressed under weights, and finally hung to dry with air. The technique seems to have originated in the Arab world, then found its way to ancient Greece and ended up in Italy for sublimation. The fish of choice for Italian *bottarga* making is mullet—in Sardinia and for that small hyperlocal production in the town of Orbetello where I first encountered it—and tuna—in coastal Sicily. Their flavors are quite different; the salinity of mullet *bottarga* has a citrusy profile and a lingering bouquet that ends in

the nose, while *bottarga* from tuna roe has a flashy and immediate briny fishiness. Mullet *bottarga* is a larger and more distributed production. The tuna one needs a little scouting, even in Italy. I love and keep both in my pantry, but if I were forced to choose, it would be mullet, the one that first defined *bottarga* to my palate.

Bottarga has enjoyed increasingly well-deserved notoriety throughout the years, starting with chefs and eventually becoming easy to find online and in specialty stores. Not all Italian *bottarga* is created equal. While the majority is still transformed in Sardinia and Sicily, the raw material often comes from other seas. The few still responsible and sustainable local productions create a superior product that's at once prohibitive and worth every penny.

Bottarga is available in whole pieces or grated in jars. Whole pieces are sold still wrapped in the sac's membrane, which locks in the moisture and maintains the flavor intact. Peel only the amount you are planning to use, then enfold it back in the membrane to store in the refrigerator. The essence of *bottarga* somewhat volatilizes when grated, so its flavor is drier and shorter but still holds the essence of the sea. In both forms, *bottarga* will last a long time refrigerated.

There is no reason to cook this sea sprite dust. In fact, one shouldn't. *Bottarga* is a finish over dishes made of clean, simple ingredients. It is the unexpected guest that will make your evening a lasting success and you will end up inviting over and over.

Celery root is like motherhood for me. I got to it late and without a plan, but I can no longer envision days without it. I eat celery root raw or roasted, poached or pureed, stewed or shredded. Its flavor is cindery and slightly sour but also sweet and toasty—all profiles that pair to a T with the essence of bottarga. Chervil is ethereally suited to celery root, but parsley or tarragon will also do. And if dairy is not for you, leave out the crème fraîche and swirl with a little olive oil instead. Last but not least, I always have vermouth in my liquor cabinet, as it is one of my preferred aperitivi, but white wine can be substituted.

Vellutata di sedano di Verona con bottarga
Celery root soup with bottarga

To expeditiously clean the celery root, trim off a thin slice from both the top and the bottom. Rest the celery root on one of the now flat ends. Peel off the tight, gritty gnarl in strips with a sharp chef's knife, following the contour of the root from the top to the bottom. Pare any leftover grit patches with a small knife. Rinse the celery root and cut it into small chunks.

Finely chop the shallot. Save a few chervil tips for garnishing and mince the rest. Grate 1½ teaspoons zest from the orange.

Pour half of the olive oil into a saucepan over medium-low heat. When its fragrance wafts up to your nostrils, add the shallot, chervil, zest, and 1 teaspoon salt. Sauté for 5 to 6 minutes, until the shallot is tender and hazy.

Raise the heat all the way up and add the chunks of celery root. Stir for a couple of minutes to coat in the shallot and lemon yumminess, then douse with the vermouth. Stand by the stove until the fumes of the alcohol turn from punching your nose to caressing your eyes.

Pour warm water into the pan until the celery root is covered by about 1 inch / 2.5 cm. When the water comes to a boil, turn down the heat to a simmer. Cook for another 20 to 25 minutes, until the celery root is soft enough to be mashed.

Puree the soup with a handheld blender while streaming in the remaining olive oil. If the soup is too thick for your liking, add a little more warm water.

Sample a spoonful and adjust with salt and season with white pepper to your taste. Ladle the soup into warm cups or bowls. Swirl in small dollops of crème fraîche, generously fleck with bottarga shavings, and garnish with the reserved chervil. Serve hot.

MAKES 4 CUPS / 950 ML; FOR 2 TO 4 PEOPLE

1 celery root, just a little over 1 pound / 450 g

1 small shallot

¼ cup / 5 g loosely packed chervil leaves

1 orange

½ cup / 120 ml extra-virgin olive oil

Salt and white pepper

½ cup / 120 ml dry vermouth

2 tablespoons crème fraîche

3 tablespoons mullet bottarga shavings

This three-ingredient dazzler is a party starter that requires a little technique, which I learned from my colleague and friend Corrado Sani, a San Francisco Bay Area–based Florentine chef. Because it must be served warm and creamy, I make the batter in advance and apply said technique as guests are sipping and schmoozing in the kitchen. Invariably the conversation sparkles until your audience's taste buds are stunned into silence upon first tasting. Crème fraîche best ticks the tang-to-fat box, but heavy cream, sour cream, or even buttermilk will work.

Uova in crema alla bottarga di tonno
Creamed eggs with tuna bottarga

FOR 6 TO 8 PEOPLE

3 eggs

3 tablespoons
crème fraîche

Salt and white pepper

1½ teaspoons
unsalted butter

2 to 3 tablespoons
grated tuna bottarga

Set up a double boiler by inserting a heatproof bowl into a pot in which it fits snugly without touching the bottom or protruding more than 1 to 2 inches / 2.5 to 5 cm from the top. Remove the bowl, pour some water into the pot, ensuring it will not come into contact with the bowl, and replace the bowl. Set the double boiler on the stove to gently heat the water.

Meanwhile, break the eggs into another bowl and plop in the crème fraîche. Whisk them until they are uniform in color. Sniff the mixture, then add ¼ teaspoon salt. Sniff again; the fresh sulfur of the eggs and tang of the crème fraîche should be more detectable. If necessary, whisk in a little more salt until the balance of the aromas pleases your nose. Season with a pinch of white pepper, then whip a little more, just to fluff the batter with a bit more air.

Adjust the heat so the water stays at a low simmer, then add the butter to the bowl and wait until it has melted. Tilt the bowl with the egg mixture over the double boiler and let the batter descend in a thread onto the butter while whisking it continuously. Do not stop whisking; within 2 to 3 minutes, the mixture will start setting and then becoming a richly smooth and thick custard.

Turn off the heat and spoon the custard into tiny bowls. I use 2-tablespoon / 30-ml glass bowls. Sprinkle generously with the bottarga and serve warm with a demitasse spoon.

Because of its richness, this dish can spoil the appetite if eaten in large amounts. You should give just a tiny taste—or two at most—to sharpen your guests' desire for the meal to come.

At fifteen, my larger-than-life mother crossed paths with a red-haired, gold-eyed beauty. Her name was Milla—short for Camilla—and she summered in the same town where my family has owned a place since the 1950s. It was an instant friendship that lasted a lifetime, and to this day carries between my sisters and me and zia Milla's daughters. A love of and aptitude for good cooking were one of the threads my mother and Milla shared. Memories of her casual kitchen instincts still inform my cooking. From her, I learned that octopuses are tastier if you leave their small brains in, and that bottarga delivers such flavor, you need to do very little to it.

The caftan-clad zia Milla would swish into the kitchen, and in the fragments of time she'd steal from espresso sipping and Marlboro puffing, she'd string together the magic that would mesmerize me later that day at the table. This recipe is the story of how she could make both bottarga and a summer evening sparkle.

Spaghetti alla bottarga della zia Milla
Aunt Milla's spaghetti with bottarga

A couple of hours before dinner, shave the bottarga paper-thin and spread it in a shallow serving bowl in one layer. Grate 2 teaspoons zest from the lemon, then squeeze 2 teaspoons juice. Sprinkle the juice all over the bottarga, then scatter the zest.

Chop the parsley leaves finely and dust them on the bottarga slices.

Smash the garlic clove with the side of a chef's knife, then slide it out of its skin. Toss it into the serving bowl. Season with pepper to suit your palate. Drown the bottarga in the olive oil and go get all shellacked for your guests.

While waiting for the gang to arrive and before putting heels on, stack plates and forks on the kitchen counter, then fill a tall pot with 4 quarts / 4 L water and set it on the stove.

While the aperitivo glasses are clinking and the laughter is reverberating across the living room into the kitchen, turn the heat on under the pot to bring the water to a boil. While the water heats, join the living room fun.

FOR 6 PEOPLE

4-ounce / 115-g piece mullet bottarga (about 1 whole piece)

1 lemon

½ cup / 10 g loosely packed parsley leaves

1 garlic clove

Black pepper or red chili flakes

¼ cup / 60 ml extra-virgin olive oil, plus more for finishing

Salt

1 package (1 pound / 450 g) spaghetti

continued

Spaghetti alla bottarga, continued

By the time you visit the kitchen again for gin-and-tonic refills, the water will be boiling. Season it with 1½ tablespoons salt, drop in the spaghetti, stir, and cover the pot. Set a timer for 1 minute shy of the suggested cooking time. Refill the glasses and remove the lid from the pot, since the water is now back to a boil. Adjust the heat so the water is at a lively, but not rolling, boil.

When the timer goes off, motion everyone to follow you into the kitchen. Move the spaghetti out of the water with tongs and lead them straight into the bottarga bowl while they are still steaming hot.

Toss and swirl with glee while your guests are getting a plate. If the spaghetti seem a little dry, loosen the strands with a spoonful or two of the pasta cooking water.

Stack yarns of spaghetti onto the plates of your friends, leaving the friend you like best for last—the bottom of the pasta bowl always has the most sauce.

No need for wine. A gin and tonic works wonderfully with spaghetti alla bottarga.

I am uncharacteristically proud of this creation, which I concocted for a food trade conference during which I was given the task of stretching the audience's imagination on what to do with Italian ingredients. Artichokes and bottarga are a match I discovered when I worked at a famed New York restaurant in the very early days of my cooking career. Pork tenderloin has the subtle flavor and suited texture of a good backdrop, and orange zest is the zing that cinches it all.

Filetto di maiale con carciofi e bottarga di muggine
Pork tenderloin with artichokes and mullet bottarga

Season the pork generously with salt and leave it on the counter to come to room temperature.

Fill your salad spinner with cold water. Cut the lemon in half and squeeze the juice into the water. Drop in the drained lemon halves.

Pick up the first artichoke and remove the outer leaves until about two-thirds of the outer circle of leaves are a lighter, somewhat yellowish green. Slice off the darker top tips of the leaves close to the top,, being mindful of the thorns. Pare the outer part of the bottom and peel the stem. Finally, slice off a very thin layer from the bottom of the stem. This procedure is called turning, as for each phase of it, your knife will circle around the artichoke.

Cut the turned artichoke in half lengthwise and remove the choke if necessary. The choke is that hay-like fuzz that is often, but not always, in the middle of an artichoke. Cut each half lengthwise into thin slices and drop them into the lemon water to prevent oxidation. Repeat with the remaining artichokes. Rub your hands and fingers with the lemon halves all over to remove the bitterness, then wash them well with soap and water. Do not forgo this last step, lest the bitter residue travels to other ingredients your hands will touch.

Mince together the shallot and half of the parsley leaves with a generous pinch of salt into a paste.

FOR 4 TO 6 PEOPLE

1 pork tenderloin, about 1½ pounds / 680 g

Salt and pepper

1 lemon

3 medium-size artichokes

1 small shallot

½ cup / 10 g loosely packed parsley leaves

½ cup / 120 m extra-virgin olive oil

1 cup / 240 ml dry white wine

2 to 3 tablespoons grated mullet bottarga

½ tablespoon grated orange zest

Freshly ground black pepper, for the dressing

continued

Filetto di maiale con carciofi e bottarga di muggine, continued

Pour 2 tablespoons of the olive oil into a frying pan over low heat, add the parsley and shallot mince, and cook, stirring often so it doesn't burn, for 5 to 7 minutes, until soft, fragrant, and hazy.

Meanwhile, lift the basket out of the salad spinner, discard the water, and spin the artichokes to shake off the excess moisture.

Raise the heat under the frying pan to medium-high and toss in the artichokes. Season with salt and pepper and continue to sauté, swirling the pan often, for about 20 minutes, until the artichokes are tender. If they stick, add a bit of warm water. When the artichokes are ready, sample them and season them with salt and pepper to suit your taste. Turn off the heat and cover the pan to keep them warm.

While the artichokes are cooking, heat the oven to 400°F / 200°C / gas mark 6.

Pat the pork tenderloin dry. Pour 3 tablespoons / 45 ml of the olive oil into an ovenproof sauté pan large enough to hold the pork and place it over medium heat. When the oil shimmers and slithers and you can smell it without bending over the stove, add the meat and brown it lightly on all sides, remaining mindful every time you turn it to not forcefully pull the meat away from the pan before it releases easily. Raise the heat to high, pour in the wine, and deglaze the pan, stirring to scrape up any brown bits from the pan bottom.

When the wine no longer makes you wince with acidity but rather caresses you with sweetness, slide the pan into the hot oven. Roast the tenderloin until it reaches an internal temperature of 125°F / 52°C. It should take 10 minutes at most.

Use an oven mitt to remove the pan from the oven and tongs to move the pork to a wire rack to cool. When you put the pan in the sink, please leave the mitt around it to be sure that everybody is aware of its temperature.

Tip the bottarga into a bowl, add half the zest, and whisk in the last 3 tablespoons of olive oil to make a dressing. Season with freshly ground pepper to best suit your palate. Chop the remaining half of parsley leaves.

By now, the pork tenderloin should be juicy, ever so slightly pink in the center, and a perfect warm room temperature. Slice it thinly at a slight slant and arrange the slices on a warm platter in concentric circles. Top with the warm artichokes, drizzle the bottarga dressing over everything, and dust with the chopped parsley and remaining zest. Serve at room temperature.

The pleasing nature of ricotta makes it a well-suited canvas for the marked personality of bottarga. I've paired them in this unusual pasta with fragrances that seem unexpected but that underscore and harmonize the traits of both ingredients. Since the dressing requires no cooking, it is ideal on a hot summer day. If trofie aren't available in your area, you can use fusilli or penne.

Trofie con ricotta e bottarga di muggine al profumo di arancio
Trofie with orange-scented ricotta and mullet bottarga

FOR 5 TO 6 PEOPLE

1 small orange

1 marjoram sprig

6 ounces / 170 g ricotta

Salt and pepper

Nutmeg, for grating

½-piece mullet bottarga, 2 to 3 ounces / 60 to 90 g

Extra-virgin olive oil as needed

1 package (1 pound / 450 g) trofie

Fill a pot with 3 quarts / 3 L water, cover it, and set it over heat to come to a boil.

While the water is heating, grate the zest from half of the orange. Pick a few pretty marjoram tips for garnishing, then strip the leaves off the sprig and mince them.

Combine the ricotta, minced marjoram, orange zest, and ½ teaspoon salt in a serving bowl. Stand over the bowl and grate nutmeg into it until your nose can detect its fragrance. Stir well.

The water should be boiling by now. Season it with 1½ tablespoons salt, stir in the trofie, and cover the pot. Set a timer for 1 minute shy of the suggested cooking time. When the water starts to boil again, remove the cover and adjust the heat so the water is at a lively, but not rolling, boil.

While the pasta cooks, shred the bottarga into a small bowl and barely cover it with olive oil. Loosen the ricotta mixture with 3 to 4 tablespoons / 45 to 60 ml of the pasta cooking water.

When the timer goes off, fish the pasta out of the water with a handheld strainer and mix it well with the ricotta. Add the bottarga and olive oil and mix again. If it seems dry, you can loosen it with a bit more pasta water. Season with pepper to suit your taste.

Garnish with the marjoram tips and serve right away.

While the skeleton of a book to help people find space in their home cooking for the amazing food crafts of Italy has been clacking in the background for some time, the flesh to those bones came during the COVID lockdown. Cooking at home became inescapable and, after a while, a chore even to someone who loves cooking as much as I do. I had to look for shortcuts to impart the deep flavors I crave in my food while reducing daily time in the kitchen.

This non-recipe is a child of that odd time. It is a last-minute dish for me, and unless I have cooked beans in the refrigerator, I unashamedly resort to a good can of beans. And while the photo next to this recipe has bottarga shavings, I use already grated from a jar when the day has been long and I want to spend no more than fifteen minutes making dinner.

Cannellini e bottarga
Cannellini and bottarga

Drain and rinse the beans. Smash and peel the garlic clove. Grate 1 teaspoon zest from the lemon.

Combine the olive oil, garlic, and zest in a small frying pan and set over medium-low heat. Stand by the stove until the combined fragrance of the three ingredients wafts up to your nostrils.

Add the beans and swirl and sauté in the pan until they are thoroughly heated; it should take 5 minutes at the most, and if it seems like they are sticking, add a splash of water. Sample the beans and season with salt and pepper to suit your palate.

Divide the beans among three plates, then top with the bottarga, either shaved by you or grated spooned straight from a jar. Finish with a drizzle of olive oil and the lemon zest, and serve.

FOR 3 PEOPLE

1 can (14 ounces / 400 g) cannellini beans

1 garlic clove

1 lemon

2 tablespoons extra-virgin olive oil, plus more for finishing

Salt and pepper

2-ounce / 60-g piece mullet or tuna bottarga, or 2½ tablespoons grated

1 teaspoon grated lemon zest

shopping sources

SHOPPING LOCALLY

Every place I have visited in the United States had an Italian deli, and, invariably, it was a trove of well-priced staples. So wherever you are, find and befriend your Italian grocer. I must give a special mention to the Arthur Avenue covered market in the Bronx, to Brooklyn's Coluccio, and Market Hall in Berkeley, CA. Buon'Italia in the Chelsea Market in Manhattan and Di Palo's in New York City's Little Italy will both ship to you if you don't live in the area. If you live in one of the cities that boasts an Eataly, you are in for a one-stop-Italian-food-shopping adventure, but you can also find Italian food crafts in specialty stores and high-end supermarkets.

ONLINE

$$$

gustiamo.com (anchovies, balsamic, bottarga, capers, caper berries, and caper leaves, coffee, farro, legumes, olive oil, olives, nuts, pasta, rice, tomatoes, including Piennolo, Corbarini, and estratto)

177milkstreet.com (flours, grains, pasta, spices, tomatoes, wild herbs)

giadzy.com (tomatoes, Artemide black rice, anchovies, pasta)

formaggiokitchen.com (cheeses)

diasporaco.com (black and white pepper, specialty spices)

eataly.com (Italian pantry and fresh provisions)

$$

ritrovo.com (olive oil, olives, pasta, tomatoes)

casadecase.com (bottarga, capers, cheese in bulk, farro, guanciale, olives, pancetta, pasta, polenta, rice, sea salt, spices)

almagoumet.com (PDO and PGI Italian pantry and fresh provisions)

$

madeineatalia.com and supermarketitaly.com (online Italian supermarkets with inexpensive pantry basics)

Specialty products

buyportuguesefood.com (baccalà)

mrespresso.com (coffee beans for espresso)

US PRODUCERS OF GOOD ITALIAN STAPLES

Tomatoes
Di Bianco

Cereals
Anson Mills
Bayview Pasta
Community Grains
Semolina Artisanal Pasta
Sfoglini Pasta
Boulder Pastificio
Bluebird Grains Farm

Fresh Cheese
Angelo e Franco
Gioia Cheese
Bellwether
Ramini Mozzarella

Salumi
Canteen Meats
La Quercia
Cesare Casella

Bottarga
Cortez

acknowledgments

To all my fellow Italians who craft good foods, who steward our land, who keep communities tightly knit, all the while thrilling the world's palates, and keeping wanderers like me grounded: remember that your work is invaluable even when it seems impossible.

Leslie Jonath—you are the condition sine qua non of this book. I love you, my agent extraordinaire and irreplaceable friend.

Shakirah Simley—infinitely inspiring, unerringly real human being. There would be no book without those three magic words your love nonchalantly tossed my way: "ITALY BY INGREDIENT." "That's who you are" you continued. It seems you were right.

Molly DeCoudreaux—best photographer ever. You got behind the lens, unflappingly heeded to my styling opinions even when you couldn't find their sense, and artfully brought my middle-age quirks to life.

Ashley Lima—my art director, thank you for calmly dealing with the tight deadlines and the constant vortex of ideas. You made my vision shine on the page even better than it did in my head.

Tori Ritchie—friend, mentor, fairy godmother, you've been there since day one and at every critical juncture. I appreciate it more than I can ever express.

Victorine Lamothe—my champion at Rizzoli who gleaned the worth of this project even before it was fully fleshed.

Sharon Silva—my respectfully skilled and deeply knowledgeable editor. Thank you for patiently working around my flights of linguistic and grammatical fancy.

The very best Italian Consuls General a community can have—Fabrizio Marcelli (2008–2012), Mauro Battocchi (2012–2016), Lorenzo Ortona (2016–2021), and Sergio Strozzi (2021 to present) for always supporting my work and appreciating my food. Especially my friend Lorenzo, who went as far as honoring me with a knighthood. Since 2020 I hold the title of Cavaliere dell'Ordine della Stella d'Italia.

Rosie Branson Gill—thank you for being the first to swing the cooking classroom door open.

Jen Nurse and Theresa Salcedo—I hope you keep welcoming me into that classroom until my body gives. You are the kind of colleagues we all should aspire to be and the kind of friends everyone needs.

My culinary inspirations—you are all mentioned and credited throughout the stories I tell and the recipes I share. Thank you so so much.

Paolo Buitoni and Livia Stefanini—my parents, who brought me into this world, taught me to look at it differently. Though they exited the stage way too early, they are still protagonists in my life story.

Filippo, Silvia, Camilla, Giulia—my siblings, I stand at the center of the four cardinal points you anchor.

Benedetta, Giovanni, Ruggiero, Livia, Paolo, Francesco, and Bianca—my nieces and nephews. I love you and would do anything for you. My door will always be wide open.

My large and beloved family of aunts, uncles, cousins, more nieces, and more nephews—you bring me back to reality so that I can fly even higher.

My friends—the earth under my wandering feet. I am lucky that you are many. You know who you are and where you stand.

To all the home cooks whom I teach and from whom I learn—you are instrumental in honing my craft and shaping my voice. I wouldn't be who and how I am without you to make me believe there is worth in what I do.

Cristina Williams, Jennifer Gallop, Linda Tay, Beatrice Meredo, Alessandra Cassar, Jennifer Braun, Ray Ryan, Lucia Coronel, Bobby Lombardi, Chiara Andres, Marina Lombardi, Barbara D'Aloisio, Elisabetta Ghisin, Mara Roccaforte, Catherine Dauer, Paige Webster Teeple, Bebe Carminito, Anna Voloshyna, Tori Ritchie—thank you for testing my recipes!

A special thank you to Francesca Sossi for taking on the whole baccalà chapter.

John Fox—father, husband, lovebear. You show up last because you are the foundation that makes everything possible. I had to close my eyes when you first kissed me in that Tribeca elevator, the light emanating from the rest of my life was blinding.

index

Italy by Ingredient
Artisanal Foods, Modern Recipes

First published in the United States of America in 2023 by
Rizzoli International Publications, Inc.
300 Park Avenue South
New York, NY 10010
www.rizzoliusa.com

Photographs by Molly DeCoudreaux

Publisher: Charles Miers
Editor: Victorine Lamothe
Production Manager: Maria Pia Gramaglia
Managing Editor: Lynn Scrabis

Editorial Packaging and Design:
Leslie Jonath and Ashley Lima, Connected Dots Media

Printed in Hong Kong

2023 2024 2025 2026 / 10 9 8 7 6 5 4 3 2 1

ISBN: 978-0-8478-7364-7
Library of Congress Control Number: 2023932257

Visit us online:
Facebook.com/RizzoliNewYork
Twitter: @Rizzoli_Books
Instagram.com/RizzoliBooks
Pinterest.com/RizzoliBooks
Youtube.com/user/RizzoliNY
Issuu.com/Rizzoli